INSTRUMENTS OF RELIGION AND FOLKLORE

Fifteenth century psaltery, played with quills

By the same author

INSTRUMENTS OF POPULAR MUSIC

INSTRUMENTS OF PROCESSIONAL MUSIC

St. Paul's Cathedral, north case. Smith-Wren, 1695–1696

A History of Musical Instruments

INSTRUMENTS
OF RELIGION
AND FOLKLORE

LILLA M. FOX

with drawings by the author

1 290456

LUTTERWORTH PRESS · LONDON

First published 1969
COPYRIGHT © 1969 BY LILLA M. FOX

Acknowledgements

I WOULD LIKE to acknowledge the help given by Coventry Cathedral Council; the English Folk Dance and Song Society and the Vaughan Williams' Library; the Horniman Museum and Library; Robin Morton of the Ulster Folk Music Society; the Northern Ireland Tourist Board; Mr. C. Nuttall, organist of Reigate Parish Church; the Salvation Army Museum and Director of Publicity; Mr. A. Shelton, Captain of the Ringers, Reigate Parish Church; and lastly to fellow members of the Galpin Society, of which I have the honour to be a member.

L. M. F.

7188 1374 X

Printed in Great Britain by
Cox & Wyman Ltd., London, Fakenham and Reading

Contents

	Acknowledgements	4
	Introduction	7
1	HISTORY	13
2	BELLS	35
3	ORGAN	47
4	STRINGS	68
5	WOODWIND	78
6	FLUTES AND WHISTLE PIPES	85
7	FREE REEDS	90
8	PERCUSSION	94
9	BRASS	103
10	INSTRUMENTS OF THE BIBLE	114
	List of Books	120
	APPENDIX: *The Scales*	121
	List of Useful Organizations	122
	Museums and Collections	122
	List of the Stops on Coventry Cathedral Organ, 1962	123–24
	List of the Stops on St. Paul's Organ, 1697	125
	A Ringers' Rhyme	126
	A Medieval Latin Rhyme about the Bell	126
	Index	127

Morris Dancers

Introduction

TO MANY PEOPLE religious instrumental music means an organ in church, sometimes so indifferently voiced as to suggest a herd of galumphing elephants thickly overlaid with syrup; while the music of folklore is no more than the memory of a shrill pipe and funny little drum played by a gentleman wearing a flowery hat and cricket gear tied up with ribbons while others similarly attired dance round with bells below their knees. Yet at the beginning of known history men danced mystical ring dances and used noise-makers, such as the knock of metal on metal, to frighten evil spirits from their sacred ritual. The organ started its long career in ancient Rome, playing at the Coliseum where took place such spectacles as throwing Christians to the lions.

The earliest and most primitive of instruments are the noise-makers;

Hungarian long flute   *Rumanian Bucium, or wooden trumpet*

rattles, stamping tubes and sticks—the Australian lagerphone, a stick with jingling bottle tops on it is one—and later, primitive drums of all sorts. These are rhythmic noise-makers. The next class are non-rhythmic: scrapers, bullroarers and ribbon reeds. All these are and have been used in ritual dances and ceremonies connected with magic; magic denotes the means by which primitive man tried to influence forces he did not understand; rainmaking, for instance, or ritual to make fertile the animal on which he depended for food.

Powerful magic was connected with wind instruments. Flutes are still played as a love charm in parts of Europe, a remnant of their part in fertility rites; they are male instruments, and the various peasant flutes of Hungary may only be played by men to this day. In some parts of the world the long trumpets of wood or metal were played by the shamans (holy men); even now, in certain Amazonian tribes, a woman who has seen the sacred trumpets is killed. In parts of Rumania wooden trumpets are still blown by women at sunset, the time of day when, long ago, magic was worked to ensure the re-appearance of the sun or a sacred star.

Magic was connected with the stringed instruments, among the earliest being the ground harp and ground zither, in both of which the soundbox is a pit with a bark lid. Musical bows, which need a gourd, tin can, or the player's mouth as a resonator, are not connected with hunting ritual, but sometimes with rituals of women, and communion with spirits. The old Scots ballad about the drowned girl whose breastbone was made into a harp has its counterpart in an African legend about a drowned girl made into a musical bow. The lyre of the later civilization of ancient Greece was a divine instrument played by the god Apollo.

Instruments had a deeper magic than their part in ritual. The very fact that a hollow bone, a ribbon of reed, or a whirled blade made a loud sound could mean that they were possessed by a supernatural force, a spirit or a god. The holy trumpets of Tibet are the very breath of a god himself. In parts of East Africa the drums were considered so holy that the yard of their dwelling place gave sanctuary to fugitives. The playing of a sacred instrument was an integral part of the religious ritual and often the most important of all, the presence of the god.

Some Fathers of the Early Christian Church gave religious symbolism to the instruments of the Psalms, the singing of which was and is so important a part of the worship of both Christian and Jew. Thus, commenting on Psalm 150, Origen, in the early third century interpreted the harp as "the soul moved by Christ's command"; the timbrel as moral discipline (this was to have an interesting echo in the nineteenth century); the stringed instruments as the harmony of virtue and the soul; the loud cymbal "the soul made prisoner by the desire for Christ"; and the high-sounding cymbal as "the pure mind informed by Christ's salvation". In

Ground bow from Uganda   *Hottentot mouth bow from Korana*

Early Grecian lyre, often made from a tortoise shell, and played with a plectrum

Slit drum from the Cameroons

the same century Eurobus of Caesarea wrote: "We sing God's Grace in spiritual songs with a living psaltery and an ensouled harp."

Pictures in later Christian MSS. show King David surrounded by the instrumentalists of their time, and may denote the religious and symbolic significance of the instruments rather than that they were played during worship. In fact, many of them fell into disrepute because of their part in theatre and circus, both condemned by the Church for distracting men's thoughts from God. After this, instruments connected with worship became the humble servants of the Church, and only the bells had supernatural powers attributed to them by virtue of their sacred office.

The little four-sided bells of the Celtic Church were believed to have the power of healing and working miracles; the bell of St. Columba on Iona was called God's Vengeance, as anyone swearing falsely on it would be cursed. The bigger bells hung in towers were christened and blessed at a special service, and given the power to ward off such evils as plague, storms, and discord among men.

In folklore, the little bells worn for certain dances of ritual origin were intended to frighten away evil spirits. Other instruments connected with folklore have long history, much of it lost for ever. Folklore itself is the survival of the religious customs and beliefs of our early ancestors: what we know about this old religion suggests a faith with a remarkable survival among country people, even to this day, although those who observe certain superstitions or customs are usually unaware of the religion and magic behind them. The priest figure on the 30,000-year-old cave painting at Lascaux in France wears the skin of a horned animal, and similar horned figures are seen again and again during history, evidence of an ancient cult of a sacred animal. Traditionally, the devil has horns. It has been said that the God of the old religion is the devil of the New: the Christians, in their missionary work all over Europe, soon found their devil; but his followers continued to worship him, in spite of much cruel and un-Christian persecution, even as late as the sixteenth and early seventeenth centuries when one of them told how they danced at night in the church-yard to the music of the Jews' trump. Most of our folk customs and some of our dances are based on this Old Faith, although in this country, instruments with any connection are few.

Instruments with a part in Christian worship are many; in fact, whole orchestras have been packed into church for special performances of religious works. This book, however, is only concerned with those which

King David playing the tuned bells
from an early 14th century MS

have played a special part in worship at various times in our history. Music is and always has been an integral part of almost all worship here, but it is the music of the human voice that is important: the instruments could be silenced, even the bells, and yet the services be held. Moreover, there have been times when instruments were held in disapproval, or even banished from worship, either because of their connection with pagan worship or the entertainment world—even now there are some people who think a guitar is out of place in church. Puritanism, a belief in a simple form of worship in which nothing must come between man and God and in which the congregation takes active part, has always either relegated instruments to the simplest of accompaniments to the singing or banned them altogether. Instrumental music, the elders considered, distracted the congregation from serious devotion, or introduced wordly and frivolous music, or led the musicians into pride in their accomplishment rather than humility in worship; all these things can be and have been true at various times. Nevertheless, instruments have always crept back, sometimes in the hands of the humblest of congregations, such as the various instruments of the musickers or church bands, and it is the loudest and most colourful of all instruments, the organ, that is most frequently found in churches, chapels and Reformed synagogues.

Tibetan trumpets (always blown in pairs)

Instruments of the Song School: organistrum, positive organ and tuned bells

1

WHEN ST. AUGUSTINE came to England in A.D. 597, he instructed his first converts in the by then well established liturgy or order of religious service; psalms, prayers and scriptural extracts were sung or chanted in the free rhythm of speech, the phrases of melody following the length of line of the words. This was called Plainsong or Plainchant, and always sung in unison. It varied in different parts of Europe, being in the West the Gregorian chant taught in Pope Gregory's Schola Cantorum (singing school) in Rome; much of it is still in use in Roman Catholic and Anglican churches. As far as we know, the first instruments allowed into worship played in unison with the plainsong, to keep the singers together and sustain the voices. These were very few: the organ was the chief, and then the organistrum for a period, and possibly bell-chimes; later, strings

11th-century bell

may have also taken part. Other instruments took part in church processions, those played by the minstrels of a bishop's entourage, for instance, while more humble minstrels joined in to play their instruments in performances of the Mysteries —the Miracle plays. There are records of organs in England as early as A.D. 700; these were simple instruments consisting of one or two ranks of whistle pipes. These were "Positive" organs, that is, were small enough to be placed in position where they were wanted. The twelfth century organistrum was a stringed instrument probably developed from the monochord. The monochord (see page 72) consisted of one string stretched over a soundbox, with bridges that could be moved to determine the exact intervals of a scale, and therefore of practical use in both singing and the study of music.

Bells came early into religious use; St. Patrick's little bell (see page 45) still to be seen in its eleventh-century shrine, is possibly fifth century. They were probably used as a call to prayer, and in 750 King Egbert ordered them to be tolled as such at the appointed times. The earliest peal of bells we know of was that of six and a tenor bell at Croyland Abbey in the tenth century. As church buildings became larger, belfries could be built to hold bells loud enough to be heard over the surrounding countryside.

The larger churches could also house larger organs. In the tenth century there was an enormous organ in Winchester Cathedral, with 400 pipes, and needing 70 men to work the bellows; it made such a noise that, according to a contemporary poem, everyone "stops with his hands his gaping ears, being in no wise able to draw near and bear the sound". This is not surprising, since there were two organists at work at once, and each slider must have controlled a large number of pipes and there was then no mechanism to stop out any of them. Few organs were as big as this; they were too costly to build and keep up, and then there were the bellows men's wages to pay. For the most part churches, and also baronial halls, were furnished with Positive organs.

Changes came into the choral music of the Church. During the eleventh century, liturgical dramas, or Mysteries, were performed. These were sung enactments of parts of the Bible, and sometimes used folk tunes and other simple music. In some cases, the congregation came to take part in them, and they were enacted outside the church; these became the medieval Miracle plays acted by the various guilds. Both Miracle plays and the liturgical drama co-existed for some time. Before that, however, music of the liturgy itself was altered: melodic passages were added to it, musical embroideries on the main theme; experiments were made with metre, since notes of different length needed some sort of metrical framework or the music was too difficult to sing. There were many experiments with poly-phony; this means many voices. Polyphonic singing was natural to the folk song of some peoples—in the eleventh century people in the North of England were found to be singing in polyphony as they still do—but did not come into Church music until the ninth and tenth centuries. The voice parts were interwoven in various ways; this contrapuntal music, as it is known, reached its height in the work of Palestrina and the Eliza-bethan composers. However, the experiments in polyphonic singing in the medieval Church were not always easy to follow, and met with disapproval. Pope John XXII issued a decree in 1325 against them, com-plaining that they made the melodies "rush round ceaselessly, intoxicating the ear without quieting it . . . and disturb devotion instead of evoking it". Later, John Wyclif, writing of the period, called them "vain tricks". However, in the present study they can help one see how instruments were brought in, first in unison with the singers, and later to take over one of the "embroideries", or to play one or more parts instead of singers.

When Bishop Lambert, Abbot of St. Bertin, visited Winchester in 1118, he was received with the sound of the famous organ and "instru-ments of concordant music"; unfortunately the chronicler does not list them, but it is likely they were played for some sort of religious procession to welcome the visitor. Various MSS. from the eighth century to the late Middle Ages show King David surrounded by instrumentalists, some of which are undoubtedly secular, and may pay homage to David as the shepherd king. Moreover, as a musician himself, he could be taken as a patron of the art, such as Apollo was in Greece; the Church was the centre of learning, and what more natural than that a treatise on music should be headed with a picture of David and attendant musicians. In the twelfth-century drawing on which this illustration is based a line is drawn literally between the sacred and the profane instruments. The king plays his harp, while instrumentalists play tuned bells, panpipes, and the finger-stopped horn now called a cornett; one musician has a song book, the bell player also has a monochord, and there are two bellowsmen ready for the organist who is presumably the figure kneeling by the king. The profane instruments are the horn, a useful and ancient instrument, the lira, associated for centuries with rustic dance, and an unusually long, barrel-shaped tabor, probably an entertainer's showpiece, played by a figure dressed in an animal's skin; it is tempting to see him a priest figure of the Old Faith, but he has no horns, and in any case, the other dancing and tumbling figures suggest entertainers, among whom were not only animal trainers but men dressed as animals. (The pantomime cat comes of a long lineage.)

In those days, the church was much more the centre of affairs than to-day, and there are written records of divines sorely tried by the noise of profane music. The nave was the meeting place for the people; the sanctuary, altar and choirstalls were in the chancel at the east end, cut off from the nave by the solid and often beautifully carved rood screen; here Mass was sung and the service carried out, and at times, the Sanctus bell rang (see page 41) to warn the people of the approach of the Holy Spirit, so that they could prostrate themselves in prayer.

Later altarpieces and stained glass windows also featured instruments, usually being played by angels; this protected them by bringing them under the cloak of the Church. Early in the Middle Ages, the minstrels had formed guilds, partly out of self protection, and partly to exercise some control over the mass of itinerant players, some of whom were rogues and vagabonds. The guilds held gatherings at cathedrals, and some-times it was obligatory for the players to light a candle for the patron saint and for the Virgin Mary, thus obtaining divine authority to practise their profession. The more wealthy minstrels, those employed by nobles and

Music Sacred and Profane, based on the 12th-century Psalter of the Abbey of
St. Remigius, Rheims
Sacred: monochord, tuned bells, organ, harp, panpipes and cornett
Profane: lira, cowshorn and barrel drum

cities, subscribed to install windows and the carved minstrels' galleries still extant in some churches and cathedrals. It does not follow that the instruments were played in worship.

The monasteries being the centres of learning, it was there that music was studied, taught, and first notated; unfortunately, only a few of the MSS. of music survive, either here or on the continent. One early fourteenth-century MS. contains variations on part of the Easter service, intended for three fiddles and more likely to have been performed for

A coven dancing in chain dance, led by the Witchmaster, or "Devil", who carries a horn. Music is provided by a shawm player

secular music than in the church itself. The art of organ building underwent many changes: a key mechanism was evolved; the ranges of notes became wider; after 1300 a type of remote control was invented so that the pipes did not need to be just above the keys, but could be arranged to look decorative and sound better. After 1400, stop mechanisms enabled the player to stop out various ranks of pipes, leaving others to sound alone; this was of immense importance, as now differently voiced pipes could alternate with each other, and organ music became colourful as well as powerful. Later still, reed pipes as well as whistle, or flue, pipes were added. Only cathedrals and large churches could afford a Great organ, but many had more than one Positive, sometimes called the Quire or Chair organ.

Nobles and princes often had their own chantries, or chapels; 'chapel' originally meant the place of worship, but later also meant the clergy and musicians in the service of the important personage. The chief of these was the Chapel Royal; there are records of its activities as early as 1135, and over the centuries many musicians were trained under its auspices, and composers were attached to it. All other private chantries were forbidden during the Reformation under Edward VI, the Chapel Royal alone continuing to provide patronage for musicians, and many of the great composers of the English Renaissance composed for it at one time and another. The continental equivalent, also associated with many great names, were the Cappellae or Kappells.

It must be remembered that while the cathedrals, the monastic and larger churches could have choirs, complete with "singing boys" and choir schools, and organs and other instruments, there were up and down the country, many little churches, remote, poorly endowed, and served by a parish priest obliged to till his bit of land like any peasant, and knowing enough of Church music to chant the liturgy and perhaps train up a few boys and men to help out. In such places, too, the Old Faith was probably more widespread than we are used to think. A few remaining traditional dances of ritual origin, such as the Abbott's Bromley Horn dance, are danced at certain times of year, and some traditional animals like the Padstow and Minehead Hosses still appear, as they have done as far back as we know. As far as we know, too, they danced to the music of whistle and reed pipes, later pipe and tabor, and the Jews' harp, while the noise-makers had a place in various old rites and customs.

The Reformation started in Saxony in 1517 when Martin Luther openly voiced the doubts and aspirations of many religious people. He did not wish to divide the Catholic Church, then the only Church in Western Europe, but to reform it; nor to suppress the Mass, only to delete parts he thought irreligious, and to translate it into the vernacular—the language of the people—so that they could understand and participate in the service. To this end he favoured singing in which they could join, and himself set to music psalms and texts, publishing a book of them in 1524; music, he believed, was the gift of God, and rightly used in worship.

However, the Church could not contain the new thought and learning; some of Luther's followers formed the Lutheran Evangelical Church, its teaching based on the Gospel—evangelist means preacher of the Gospel. Others, under his disciple John Calvin, founded a stricter section, the Reformed Churches, well-organized bodies with presbyters (priests) of equal status sharing the work of the Church with the laity; the established Church of Scotland is one of these. Their services were more simple, with congregational psalm singing, unaccompanied by any musical instrument.

In England, the Reformation came slowly. When Henry VIII broke with the Pope he preserved the order of the Mass and the Church services as they had been, but Protestants in the Church preached the need for a simpler service in which the congregation could take active part. When Edward VI became king, the powers behind the throne were Protestant, and instituted many changes. In 1538, Bibles in English were put into the churches for all to read; these were chained to their lecterns, and some can still be seen. In 1549 the first English Prayer Book appeared, the *Boke of Common Praier*, with a simplified Mass in English. Some of Luther's music was adopted, and soon after the publication of Elizabeth's English Prayer Book ten years later, a book of metrical psalms was published for congregational singing. It was not easy to join in the singing of the plainsong, nor the complicated polyphony that had grown round it, nor the beautiful Masses written for the Church by such composers as Tye and Tallis. The psalms, some of the most beautiful religious poetry ever known, had always been most important to both Christian and Jewish worship, and the Protestants, wishing to restore them to congregational singing, put them into simple four-line verse metre sung to simple easily learned tunes. Some of the tunes were poor, and the verses doggerel, but others are still sung, such as the 23rd Psalm and Old Hundredth, so-called because it was the setting of Psalm 100 in the Old Standard Edition of the book.

In 1592 Este published a *Whole Booke of Psalms* with four-part harmonies, the tunes being named after towns and villages in the British Isles; some of these, too, can be found in modern hymn books. Other books were published and some people made private collections of psalm tunes, old and new, and of hymns, which are devotional songs not necessarily based on the Scriptures. Some of the latter were beautiful, as poetry and as music. The music of Wither's Hymns and Songs of the Church (1623) was written by Orlando Gibbons.

In the early days of the Reformation in England, when the private chantries were forbidden, many of them were despoiled and their organs destroyed along with other church furniture. (Church furniture means the inside fittings of a church.) There was a decree against the ringing of bells, except just before the sermon. In 1563 a petition drawn up by some of the more extreme Protestants—or Puritans as they were becoming to be known—asking among other things that 'all curious singing and playing of the organs be removed' was narrowly defeated in Parliament, while in 1552 the Archbishop of York had commanded "that there be

Early 16th-century treble viol

Later 16th century tenor viol

no more playings of the organs". In fact, although the Church was still one under the Crown, it was already splitting up into the diversity of religious sects of later times. During the long reign of Elizabeth, services varied according to the prevailing beliefs of priest and congregation.

The Renaissance gave rise to a great flowering of the human spirit all over Europe; it was seen here in the poets and dramatists, and the composers and musicality of the people during the Elizabethan age. In many churches and cathedrals, and in the Chapel Royal—the queen herself was in her private worship what we now term High Church—there was much "curious singing". This included the incomparable choral work of such masters as Tallis, Byrd and Gibbons, both Masses and settings of the psalms and other parts of the liturgy. They also composed anthems; these were the Protestant version of the old Latin Motets, or *Cantiones Sacrae* (sacred songs) and were extracts from the Scriptures set for part singing; they were peculiar to the Anglican Church. They were supposed to be unaccompanied, but organ or viols often played in unison with the various parts. The cornett was played in church, usually with the sacbut for the bass part. Organs were not only played in church, but for those who could afford a Positive, then known as a Chamber organ, in private houses and taverns. Organ music was composed which suggests that, although they were not as advanced as those in Germany, they were sweet-voiced and responsive.

Church bells were rung again, and new bells cast. A visitor, Paul Hentzner, wrote in the mid-sixteenth century: "The people of England are vastly fond of great noises . . . such as the firing of cannon, beating of drums and the ringing of bells; so that it is common for a number of them that have got a glass in their heads to get up into the belfry and ring the bells for hours together for sake of exercise . . ." At this time, ringers were ringing peals; later they took to change ringing, which is mathematical, consisting of ringing all the sequences possible to a given peal of bells. (It has been estimated that it would take thirty years' unceasing ringing to sound all the possible changes on the present twelve-bell peal in St. Paul's.)

During the reigns of the early Stuart kings, the Church became

23

increasingly anti-Puritan; both services and music became more elaborate, with professional choirs; organs; and the full complement of instruments needed for the music then coming into fashion. This was influenced by the newly-arrived Italian opera, and must have seemed to many to be both over-dramatic and worldly. Canon Peter Smart, a Protestant divine, accused a fellow-churchman, reporting that "he hath brought meere ballads and jigs into Church, and commanded them to be sung for Anthems . . . He will not suffer so much as the Holy Communion to be adminstred without an hydeous noyse of vocall and instrumentall Musicke . . ."

The Puritan tide ran very strongly, and after the civil war, church services went to the other extreme of simplicity, the Prayer Book being made illegal, and the sermon of paramount importance. Choirs and organs had no part, and the only music was the singing of metrical psalms. Extremists in the Commonwealth Army destroyed much priceless church furniture, including organs and their cases, and many bells were melted down. Outside the Church, however, serious music flourished under the Commonwealth; it was only church organs that were destroyed, others remaining in private houses and taverns; unfortunately, few of these have survived, the only one in playing order being the Positive at Carisbrooke Castle.

After the Restoration, a new Book of Common Prayer was adopted (1662) and the sung liturgy returned with choirs and organs. The music of the Chapel Royal was augmented by Charles' own musicians and re-fashioned to his taste. A contemporary wrote: "His Majesty, who was a brisk and airy Prince, was soon . . . tyred with ye grave and solemn way and ordered ye composers of his Chapell to add symphonys &c with instruments to their Anthems . . . and established a select number of his Private Musicke to play ye Symphonys and Ritornelles . . . The old Masters . . . organists to his Majesty, hardly knew how to comport themselves with these new-fangled ways . . ." Others must have had the same difficulty.

There was a shortage of trained choirs and musicians. Henry Cooke, a Royalist who had spent the Commonwealth period in Italy studying

Charles I's chamber organ at Carisbrooke castle. The bellows are worked by the foot pedal

music, became Master of the Children in the Chapel Royal; from his boys came many of the composers of the next fifty years, among them Henry Purcell.

A new school of English organ building arose, producing instruments fitted to the music of the time, and for which more music was written. These organs incorporated in one the two organs formerly used in church, the Great and the Choir or Chair, so that the organist had a manual—keyboard—for each, and could contrast the power and voices of the two. Later, a third was added, the Eccho, controlled by a third manual, but with pipes inside a box and often some way away from the others, so as

Church gallery choir and band with strings and flute

to give a faraway effect. Much care went to the design of the cases, many of which remain, even where the pipes have been altered.

There was a revival of bell ringing, and in 1688 Fabian Stedman, who had already published one book of changes, brought out *Campanology and the Art of Ringing*, a handbook giving instructions for every change in ringing bell peals from two to twelve in number; some changes still bear his name. New bells were cast, and others recast, so that many of our bells date from the late seventeenth and early eighteenth centuries.

At the same time there were a large number of dissenting sects whose members could not in conscience accept the New Prayer Book, and who were at first cruelly persecuted, as were Roman Catholics, the Mass being illegal. The services of these sects were simple, and their singing congregational. Some took their beliefs, and their singing, to extremes: the Sweet Singers of Israel, for instance, believed themselves sinless, and spent much time singing the praises of God and His Saints; the Scottish Sweet Singers rejected all authority, even that of the Bible, and went about singing certain psalms and doing as they pleased. Many of the sects faded away, leaving those based on true Christian faith, and which are still active.

Singing was their music, at first only the metrical psalms; several psalters —books of psalms—were issued during the seventeenth century, among them two Scottish and one Welsh, containing much lovely music, some still to be found in our hymn books. Later on, hymns were introduced, notably those of Isaac Watts.

Instruments were not used, apart from a pitch-pipe to give the note (see page 89), partly because they were associated with the ritual the puritans believed came between man and God, and partly because they savoured of worldliness and frivolity; also, the sects were at first poor and their meeting-houses small. By the end of the eighteenth century, many had accepted the organ to accompany the singing.

During the eighteenth century the Church of England became increasingly "latitudinarian", that is, tolerant of differences within itself, so that individual vicars had considerable freedom as to the form of worship in their churches. Some were popularly known as "squarsons", squires' sons who had taken up church livings and become parsons, with a respectable standing and an opportunity to live the life of the landed gentry; parish work was often neglected, or handed over to an underpaid curate. There were also very poor parsons, struggling to make ends meet. So while the music of cathedrals and big churches was enriched with trained choirs and new and ever-improving organs, poor or neglected churches had to get along without. In these cases, the congregation themselves often provided both choir and instrumental music, with gallery choirs and church bands. The galleries, still to be seen in a few old churches, were at the west end, so that the congregation had to turn and 'face the music', which they did gladly. The musickers, or musicianers, as the players were called, were also in the gallery, and played anything they could: fiddles, such as were played for folk dancing; oboes, flutes, and clarinets, sometimes brought home by ex-soldiers; old-fashioned violas da gamba, and 'cellos; serpents—instruments developed in France to provide a bass for church music; and almost any instrument that a musicker happened to play. They were for the most part ordinary village people, often illiterate, who put endless time and effort into their music, painstakingly learning to read and to copy out parts, repairing and sometimes making their instruments, and practising after a hard day's work and often a long walk to an unheated church. At a time when wealthier churches were playing continental church music, and hired musicians were increasingly fashionable, ordinary countryfolk played and sang the old church tunes, and kept alive the music of the people in the Church.

At the same time, the evangelical movement led by John and Charles Wesley was taking the Gospel out to the people. The Wesleys saw themselves as part of the established Church, but the movement broke away, and flourished especially in the growing industrial areas where many old Wesleyan chapels bear witness to the part they played in the lives of the labouring poor.

Charles Wesley wrote many hymns, and John had to find the tunes; he used folk tunes, melodies from older Church music, and found new composers, such as the bassoonist John Lampe. Congregational singing was a feature of the movement, accompanied only in the first place by the viola da gamba, but later, when the chapels were established, by organs, and in some places chapel orchestras like the church bands.

Organ building developed during the eighteenth century; there were a number of famous organ builders, and many of their instruments remain with their original voicing as well as their beautiful cases. The Eccho organ became the Swell having shutters at the front of its case which could be opened or closed for crescendo or diminuendo. Later, a Pedal organ was added, already an essential to much German organ music. This was yet another set of pipes, worked by foot pedals, to provide a deep-toned extra bass part.

The performance of these organs was limited, beautiful as it was; there was not the range of sound and voices available on a Bach organ. After 1830 organ builders developed a more complete "four-in-one" instrument with a full Pedal organ of six or more stops. Heavy pressure was also applied to some of the reed pipes, the first of these being known as *Tuba Mirabilis*, the Trump of Doom. Not only could these organs play all kinds of organ music, but they could make a very loud noise, and some critics called them music mills. Later developments made this name even more appropriate: in France organs had been built to play music of the Romantic period, and this approach was built into new British organs with differently voiced pipes and various higher pressures.

The Roman Catholic Church was finally emancipated in 1829. On the continent, the Reformation had resulted in a re-vitalized Catholic faith dominating many European countries, and retaining churches and cathedrals in most. A rich musical tradition grew up, with magnificent organs; choirs and choir schools; and carillons of bells that played tunes. In England, however, all but a handful of tiny chapels in out the way places, and one church, St. Etheldreda in London, were taken over by the Church of England, and Catholics had to hold their services, often secretly to avoid persecution, in chapels in private houses. Only too often the increasingly meaningless cry of "No Popery!" resulted in the destruction of Catholic property and church furniture. It was not until after the late eighteenth century that the Church of Rome was able to build churches and cathedrals here. These have organs for their music, but very often local people have prevented them from having bells other than one to call people to church.

Viola da gamba

Salvation Army band with cornets, tenor horn, baritone, euphonium, trombone, tuba and big drum

The Jewish Church had undergone a Reformation in 1810. Orthodox synagogues kept the traditional chanting of psalms and readings from the holy scrolls, led by the Cantor or Chazzan, while in the Reformed synagogues parts of the liturgy were set for choral singing with organ accompaniment. Previously, organ and instrumental music had been played at various periods in some European synagogues, and, as with the Christian churches, inferior music had been added to the service. A leader of the Reform, Sulzer, did away with much of this, preserving the beauty

and dignity of the ancient liturgy. A similar return to Plainsong has taken place in the Church of England during this century.

In the 1830s a movement started in Oxford that called for a return to the teachings and rituals of the Early Christian Church. Its followers were called Tractarians because they published a series of tracts on matters concerning the Church; they were evangelistic, sending missionaries abroad and into the slums. They revived High Church practices, and repaired and enriched many churches with new furniture, stained glass, and new or rebuilt organs. The old galleries were often pulled down, and the choirs disbanded; a new organ and organist took the place of the musickers, and choirs were trained according to the rules of the organist or a visiting music teacher. One cannot but think this polite dismissal of the old choirs and musicians almost as much a misplaced zeal as that of the iconoclastic soldiers of the Commonwealth.

The brass band movement grew up in industrial Britain under conditions that would daunt many today, and it was men trained in banding that next brought music and its instruments into the service of the Lord. These were the Salvation Army, who went into battle against sin and for salvation, using every instrument that came to hand, from Happy Eliza's violin to the guitars of the Joy Strings. They are chiefly known for their bands, establishing 400 within six years. The stirring music of brass and drum was suited to an army on the move, and proved especially attractive to those who knew no other lives than that of the slums of the late nineteenth century. Salvation Army girls played the tambourine and concertina to accompany their hymns, and any musical instrument could be turned to good account.

Early in the nineteenth century, instrument makers had been experimenting with an organ of free reeds, metal tongues that vibrate through an aperture; the mouth organ or harmonica is the simplest of these. But before the first harmonica was patented, there were many forms of small keyboard organ made under varying names, collectively known as *orgues expressifs*. In 1840 one was patented in Paris as the harmonium; it had sets of reeds of various sizes, and wind-channels that varied in bore, giving higher and lower air pressures to the reeds, so that it could have stops like a real organ. It had no pipes to take up room, and the bellows mechanism was worked by the feet. Here was an ideal instrument for the pious nineteenth-century family, for its daily prayers and hymn-singing evenings. Here too was a cheap, small instrument, easy to play and that did not go out of tune or need someone to work the bellows, and just the thing for small churches or chapels or church halls; for many people, religious music is that of the harmonium or its cousin the American organ, and not the pipe organ.

However, the pipe organ continues to be the chief accompanying instrument in places of worship. The latest are voiced so as to play both classical and romantic organ music of all European countries. Some of

Small harmonium by Alexandré 1859

them are unencased, like that at Coventry Cathedral, so the delighted listener can at least see some of the pipes that previously have been hidden away behind the diapason (the basic organ pipes and the only ones that he has hitherto been permitted to behold). Contact between the keys and pedals and the pipes is now fully electric so that the organist may be seated at the console miles away from the actual organ. There are also organs in which electric impulses make the actual sounds, and, together with all sorts of devices to make it sound like the real organ, the whole thing can be packed into a little keyboard, a box and a speaker. On the other hand, organs are being built like those of the past, for instance those played by Bach, and many organists favour a return to tracker action (see page 47) as they consider it most responsive of all.

In the Church there has been a return to the old Plainsong, and to some of the music of the Renaissance. New music has been composed for voices and organ, and many hymns for both church and chapel. Some of the greatest religious works of our times, however, works for full choir and orchestra such as Elgar's *Dream of Gerontius* or Britten's *War Requiem*, are above denomination.

Meanwhile, the traditional instruments of the people, together with their songs and dances, were almost lost. They were part of the village communities which were gradually broken down by the new industrialism and the agricultural depression. Had it not been for Cecil Sharp and his co-workers, very little of our folklore, dance and music would have survived, and the pipe and tabor and the bells of the dancers would have gone the same way as the old bagpipe and rebec, and the crwth and pibcorn which had so long a connection with the ancient music of Wales. The Welsh harp just survived, being allowed into chapel to play hymns, and in Ireland, where folk culture has a stronger hold, the Clarsach and the Uillean pipes. In our own times, there is happily a renewed and active interest in this heritage of music, some of which stretches back to the earliest religions of all.

*The Welsh harp
or Telyn*

Big Ben

2   BELLS

THE WORD "BELL" comes from the Saxon "bellan", to roar, and
although now the word applies to all sorts of bells, it originally meant only
the big bells hung in belfries of churches. They are usually made of bronze,
but sometimes from gun metal; those at Liversedge, Yorkshire, are cast
from guns captured at Genoa in 1814. Bells can weigh up to 128 hundred-
weight, the weight of Great Paul of St. Paul's, London, the largest bell
in Britain. The biggest bell of a peal is called the tenor bell; and some
cathedrals have in addition a large clock bell called the Bourdon bell,
such as Great Paul of St. Paul's. These bells are tolled at the death of

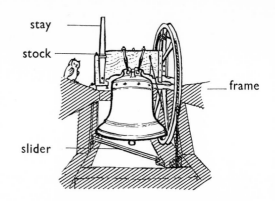

stay

stock

frame

slider

Bell in chiming position, when only a small arc is swung through. When ringing, the bell is swung almost full circle, the stay and slider preventing an "overthrow"

sovereigns. Big Ben is the best known of all, but others have more history: Great Tom of Christchurch, Oxford, has been recast several times; before the recasting in 1612, he bore the instription: "IN THOMAE LAUDE BIM BOM RESONO SINE FRAUDE" (For Thomas' sake I cry Bim Bom and no mistake). He gives 101 strokes at 9 p.m. to commemorate those who gave 101 scholarships to the college, and is also the subject of a round "Great Tom is cast". Great Paul was first cast in the reign of Edward I and called Edward of Westminster, and later Westminster Tom; he was given to St. Paul's by William III, has since been twice recast, and is tolled only on the death of Royalty, Church leaders, and Lord Mayors of London, and at 1 p.m. daily for five minutes. The Great Bell of St. Sepulchre's tolled for every execution until 1890: as the prisoners left Newgate Prison for Tyburn Gallows, the bell tolled and a bellman went ahead calling:

All good people cry heartily unto God for these poor sinners who are now going to their death!

Bells are often inscribed with their founder's name; one of our oldest bells, in Sproxton, Lancashire, cast in 1350, is inscribed: "JOHANNES DE YORKE ME FECIT IN HONORE BEATA MARIE" (John of York made me in honour of the blessed Mary). There are now only two bell foundries left in Great Britain, but there used to be many. Bells were sometimes cast by travelling foundrymen, in a field near the church; some churches

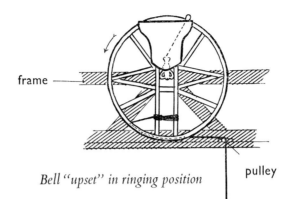

frame

pulley

Bell "upset" in ringing position

still have a Bell field or Bell lea near the church to remind them of the time when the whole village witnessed and helped with the casting and joined in the attendant ceremonies. Some were paid for by a benefactor: at Bentley Hampshire, there is a bell dated 1703 with the words:

> John Eyer gave twenty pound
> To meek mee a losty sound.

Casting and the whole making and design of bells consists of a series of delicate operations, the quality of the metal and proportions of the bell needing careful calculation.

The sound of the bell comes when the sound bow is struck by the clapper; this is called the strike note and is the keynote of the bell. It is the second harmonic (see Appendix) and at the same time six more are sounded, making the seven notes of the bell, and can be heard as the strike note dies away; of these, second, third and fourth harmonics sound the most clearly. All seven sounding together make a note called the hum note, an octave lower than the strike note and the fundamental of the harmonic scale.

—sally

Ringer ready for "hand" or "fore" stroke

The bells chime when the clapper strikes them when they are swung slightly; when they are rung, they are swung in a near circle, starting from an upside down position, with stays preventing them from swinging right over. Early wheels did not have stays, and some old bellringers called it a summerset when the bells went overturned; as it was bad for the bell, the ringers were usually fined (see Appendix). The smallest bell is always called the treble; a treble at Coventry cast in 1774 bore the words:

> Though I am but light and small
> I will be heard above you all.

The remaining bells are usually known by numbers, although in older peals they used to be christened. It is worth while to try and get up to the belfry when visiting churches, and examine the bells for inscriptions.

In this country, bells are used to ring changes; "This is an art peculiar to England," as Sir John Hawkins wrote in his *History of Music*, "and England for this reason is termed 'The Ringing Island'." Changes are all the possible sequences in which a peal of bells can be rung; there are various methods known to ringers of arranging the sequences which the captain of the ringers calls so that the other ringers know the coursing, or order of ringing. Seven hundred and twenty changes, a full peal, can be rung on six bells, 5,040 on eight, 360,000 on ten, and nearly 280 million on twelve. Some ringers consider eight a perfect peal, and others ten; with more bells the sound becomes confused.

Ringing is more than just pulling a rope; it demands training, concentration, and perfect teamwork, each ringer being motivated by the intention to make the next change better than the last. Nowadays ringers are drawn from all walks of life, especially the professional classes, and there are women captains and ringers—which would have shocked the old ringers who were, like the musickers, ordinary villagers. A gentleman wrote in 1883 that ringing was "a curious exertion of the invention and memory, and though a recreation chiefly of the lower sort of people, is worthy of notice". He should also have noticed that the ringers were very much part of the church life of the village. In many cases nowadays they are a band of devotees of the art who may have little to do with the church whose bells they ring. In the eighteenth century a French traveller wrote: "I do not suppose that there is a country where bell ringing is brought to such an art as it is here, where bells are always in chime and in harmony ... The people are so fond of the amusement that they form societies among themselves for carrying it out." Earlier ringers still, those of the seventeenth century, were often university men; Fabian Stedman, who published three books on ringing, was called the Father of the Art of Change Ringing, and was a printer in Cambridge. The oldest ringing society, founded in 1637, is called the Society of College Youths; it is still in existence, and no matter how old a ringer may be—and some have been known to ring at ninety—he is still called a Youth. Some of the earlier ringers got a bad name from playing about in the bellchamber when supposed to be ringing.

A great many bells were melted down at the Dissolution of the monasteries, so bells were newly cast, and recast, during the next three centuries, their shape being influenced by the need for the good tone and accurate tuning demanded by change-ringing.

There is a stained glass window at Ilkley church, Yorkshire, in memory of Jasper Snowdon, a famous ringer and historian, which shows the bells, wheels, ropes and all the mechanism.

In medieval times, the bells were rung in monasteries and churches by monks and clerics; they were rung to call to prayer and for the festivals of the Church. It was during the twelfth century that they were cast in their present shape; previously they had been more conical (see page 14), and their sound, according to the musicologist Curt Sachs, was "weak and whimpering". Nevertheless, some were hung in church towers, and there are records of a few peals, the earliest known being that of six bells and a tenor at Croyland Abbey in the tenth century; these were said to have made "the most exquisite music" and they were named after early saints and benefactors of the Abbey: Pega, Bega, Tatwyn, Turketyl (the Abbot responsible for their installation), Betelin, Bartholomew, and Guthlac, the tenor bell. As early as 680, the Venerable Bede wrote about a bell brought from Italy; it was in Italy that bells were first brought into the service of the Church, and the word campanology comes from the Italian name for a big bell, campana.

On the continent, especially in the Low countries, there are and have been many famous carillons, sets of bells that play tunes. Carillons originated in the little bell chimes cast by monks as early as the ninth century; these were sets of cup-shaped bells hung on a stand and struck with hammers (see page 11). They were tuned carefully, a difficult task according to early MSS., and were probably played in church, as well as in the Music Schools attached to monasteries and cathedrals, and later by secular musicians. During the thirteenth century chimes were connected up with the tower clocks so that they could play a sequence of notes at the hours and quarters; later a rotating cylinder mechanism enabled tunes to be played, and this mechanism was applied to the big bells in the tower. At this time, and as well as the carillons, clockmakers made little figures that came out and enacted scenes at each hour. During the sixteenth century the carillons were made to disconnect at will from the clock, and were given a keyboard so that a player could give performances on the bells. There are a few carillons here, but present-day conditions are un-favourable to them: at close quarters they make a jumble of sound, and one has to get some distance away to hear the tune, and then one cannot hear it for the traffic.

In 750 St. Egbert decreed "that all priests at appointed hours of day and night, do sound the bells of their churches, and they celebrate the sacred offices of God, and instruct the people". This ringing was called *signum*, a sign; it can be interpreted as a call to prayer, but can have a deeper mean-ing. The Sanctus bell rung during Mass in Roman Catholic churches is rung as a sign of the elevation of the Host at the words "*Sancte, sancte, sancte, Deus Sabaoth*" (Holy, holy, holy, Lord God of hosts) to call the congregation, who used to be outside the chancel in the nave, to prayer; so *signum* could also mean the approaching presence of the deity. The Sanctus or Sacristy bell is now a small silver handbell, but used to be a larger bell hung in a little turret on the roof, with a bell-pull in the sanctuary, so that when it was rung during Mass anyone outside should prostrate them-selves in prayer at that particularly holy time.

Bells also have powers of their own; all over the world they are and have been rung to frighten away evil spirits. The very door bell was

15-century Sanctus Bell in turret

originally hung by the door and rung to protect both dwelling and caller from the demons lurking at the threshold, a place where they were often found lying in wait. At a time when we can understand the source of so much that is harmful in our daily lives, disease, accident, or family conflict, for instance, it is easy to forget how our ancestors in the long past could only explain these things as the work of evil spirits; their lives were hedged about by these demons, and they needed charms and amulets to protect them—we still wear lucky charms. Among these bells have always been potent.

Bells, as Curt Sachs says, originally were not intended to call the church-goers but to purify the holy place. Practically all the offices of bells in the Church can be given this triple interpretation: the call to prayer, the sign of the approaching deity, and the warding off of evil. Even the curfew bell had that last meaning to our ancestors as they covered their fires and settled to sleep in the dark, well aware of the dangers outside, fire, pestilence, robbery:

> lighten our darknesse we beseche thee O Lord, and by thy great mercy defende us from all perils and daungers of this night . . .
> (The second Collect at Evensong, first "Boke of Common Praier")

41

In addition to the regular calls to prayer the bells were rung for Christian festivals, and for various local happenings. An account written in 1825 of the May Day ceremonials in Wales describes how the procession of dancers with the Cadi—the fool—and the garland bearer, "sets forth accompanied by the ringing of bells". At one time at Childermass, the Feast of the Holy Innocents, the bells used to be rung muffled, or "buffeted" with leather on the clappers. The Pancake bell was rung on Shrove Tuesday, originally a day of repentance, shrove meaning the submission of the penitent to the priest for absolution. They were rung at Hallowmass, all Hallows or All Saints; this was very important as it was then that the dead returned, not all of them friendly souls; some would flee at the sound of a church bell. The bells were and still are silent in Catholic churches from Maundy Thursday to Easter morning, in mourning for the dead Christ; at that time a still older magic was used to frighten away demons: wooden clappers or rattles. Such clappers are still used just before Easter in the Catholic Church.

There are other occasions when bells were and are rung, such as christenings, weddings, and funerals—muffled peals were sometimes rung at funerals. The Houseling bell was rung when the Eucharist was taken to a sick person, and the Passing bell as someone lay dying. "Evil spirits can't abide a Passing bell" said an old countrywoman. The ceremony of excommunication from the Church needed bell, book and candle, the bell actively casting out evil.

The bells themselves were christened, with a service of baptism, after the metal itself had been blessed in the foundry. (In some parts of the world the blood of a sacrificial victim used to be mixed in the alloy.) Baptism of bells was forbidden after a while, but the Blessing of the Bells continued until the Reformation. The bell was cleansed with holy water, and the cross on top annointed with holy oil "to make the devil flee at the sound of it". There was a long service, complete with prayers, readings and psalms, and the congregation were asked by the bishop if they believed what the Church believed concerning the holiness and virtue of bells; finally the bell was given a name. This blessing is still carried out in Catholic churches. After the Reformation a degraded form of this ceremony sometimes took place, even as late as the last century. One was described by the Rev. Gatty, author of a book on bells: it was an occasion of general rejoicing, the bell being escorted from the railway station on a decorated wagon, and stopping at the village inn to be filled with punch for all concerned. It is not surprising that the clergy put an end to this custom.

Old bells are often found to bear their name as well as that of their founder, and sometimes a coin put in during the casting; the tenor bell at Ashby, Northamptonshire, dated 1306, has a penny bearing the seal of Edward I. Often, too, there was some suitable inscription, such as that at St. Martin's in Salisbury "Be mee and loly to heare the Word of God". Another at St. Ives in Cornwall reminds the visitor that bells rung to give warning of fire could also warn of Doomsday:

> When backwards rung we tell of fire.
> Think how the world shall thus expire.

Most frequently found are the lines:

> I to the Church the living call
> And to the Grave do summon all.

The christening also conferred powers—or perhaps confirmed those powers which people already ascribed to bells—powers to quell storms, against plague and pestilence, to calm angry passions between men (see Appendix). All these powers stem from the power over evil spirits, as this extract from Wynkyn de Worde's *Golden Legend* makes clear (Wynkyn de Worde was a fellow printer of Caxton's):

> It is said, the evill spirytes that ben the regyon of th'ayre doubte moche when they here the belles rongen, and that is the cause why the belles be ringen when it thondreth, and when grete tempeste and outrages of wether happen, to the ends that the fiendes and wycked spirytes should be abashed and flee and ceese of movynge of tempeste.

The tenor bell at Malmesbury Abbey was also called the storm bell, and there are many stories of bells being rung on shore to allay storms at sea. Later, loud sound was supposed to purify the air; during a plague in 1625 a doctor ordered: "Lett the bells in cities and townes be rung often, and great ordinance discharged thereby the aire is purified."

Cow and sheep bells were originally hung round these animals' necks to protect them from demons. Handbells were rung to commemorate the dead, and in parts of Scotland the bellman used to announce deaths, sometimes being given money to pray for the soul of the departed on his "yere day", the anniversary of his death. (Handbells are now played for entertainment or for practising change ringing.) The bells of the Celtic Church had powers of performing miracles and healing; they were also believed

Handbell   *Old Wiltshire sheep bell*

to be able to move. The Celtic Church was a very old Church founded in Ireland and parts of Scotland by St. Ninian at the end of the fourth century. Early in the fifth century, St. Patrick came to Ireland and established many monasteries; from Ireland the Church spread to parts of Wales. In spite of many invasions of England in succeeding centuries, the Celtic Church continued to work and worship. It is renowned for the beauty of its surviving MSS., such as the Book of Kells, and of its stone crosses and jewelled chalices. The bells were small and made of four panels welded together, and were kept in shrines of exquisite workmanship; St. Patrick's own bell, mentioned in 552, is now in its twelfth-century shrine in Dublin.

The smaller the bell, the older the magic ascribed to it. The smallest bells of all are the jingles, tiny round bells with a metal ball inside that jingles as they move. They are sometimes seen today on children's toys and reins; they have been attached to harnesses for as long as we know, and larger bells of the same type were hung round animals' necks. During the later Middle Ages, they were worn on clothing, on hems, belts and baldricks, especially during tournaments and battles, because they were worn not for fashion but as amulets—charms against evil. This is their purpose on the legs of the Morris dancers, and other dancers of old ritual

St. Garmon's bell, Wales   *St. Moluag's 12th century bell shrine, Kilmichael Glassary, Scotland*   *St. Patrick's bell and 12th-century bell shrine*

dances in Europe. The Perth Glovers sword dancers wore 250 bells of different sizes, all over the person; sword dances are thought to stem from the ritual surrounding the first working of metal, and metal workers were held in great reverence—some, like Weland, were gods—because of their power to make such powerful things as the sword and the bells themselves.

Jingles are also worn by the fool or jester, one of the personages present in many folk dances and customs. If we go far enough back in the history of the old religions, we find that the fool was the sacrificial substitute for the king who was to be ritually sacrificed in order that his death would bring rebirth; in ancient Egypt, for instance, the blood of the sacrificed Pharaoh was sprinkled on the fields to ensure harvest. Before his death,

45

the substitute had a period when he could do anything he liked, indeed be a king, hence the fooling. But evil spirits were lurking to prevent the ritual being carried out, and the bells were there to protect him against them.

Such bells were, and still are, found on the robes of holy men in many parts of the world. In Exodus XXVIII, verses 33–35, Jehovah instructs the high priest as to his robe:

> And beneath the hem of it thou shalt make pomegranates of blue, and of purple, and of scarlet . . . and bells of gold between them round about . . . and it shall be upon Aaron to minister: and his sound shall be heard when he goeth in unto the holy place before the Lord, and when he cometh out, that he die not.

Once more the bells are seen as protection against the evil spirits that frequent thresholds.

Morris bells

SIR CHRISTOPHER WREN, referring to the organ for St. Paul's Cathedral, called it "a damned box of whistles", a summary description with a basis of truth. An organ is a box of whistles, the whistles standing inside the box, the organ case, with a reservoir of air beneath to sound them. Some of them are flue, or whistle, pipes, the sound being made by a jet of air against an edge—edge tone—as with the recorder; others are reed pipes, the sound caused by the vibrating of a metal tongue against an aperture. The reservoir in the past fed by bellows is now fed by an electric blower, and a weight set upon it equalizes the air pressure. Not only can pipes be sounded continuously, but a number can be sounded at the same time, and those of a large organ at a greater pressure than that of the human

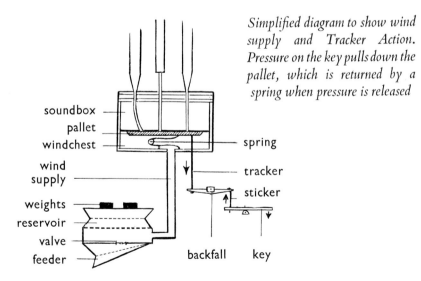

Simplified diagram to show wind supply and Tracker Action. Pressure on the key pulls down the pallet, which is returned by a spring when pressure is released

soundbox
pallet
windchest   spring
wind
supply   tracker
            sticker
weights
reservoir
valve
feeder   backfall   key

A small section of the hidden pipework of a Great Organ

lungs, so that there is sufficient volume of sound to fill a large cathedral or concert hall.

However, it was not the sound of which Wren complained. (Some of the original pipes of that organ remain in St. Paul's and their beauty of tone can still be judged) (see frontispiece). He declared that the tallest pipes would spoil the interior of his building and seven of them indeed had to be left out, the organ builder keeping them in hope that they might eventually be installed. Until the 1850s, organ builders always tried to arrange the pipes in well designed cases so that the whole enhanced the beauty of the church, but many later builders had the difficult task of fitting a large new organ into a church not built for it, and in the limited space in the chancel rather than at the west end as on the continent, so that we have a number of awkward and over-decorated cases in our churches. The pipes, as many as 3,000 of all sizes, mostly had to be stowed away behind the organ loft, often with the effect that some cannot be heard to full advantage while others boom out so that little else can be heard at all. It is interesting to see how the pipes have been installed at your local church or chapel.

The organ loft is the part where the organist sits at the console, which is the control panel. As the organ is really several organs, he will have a manual (keyboard) for each, and a pedal keyboard at his feet for the deep-toned Pedal organ. He has push-button stops or pistons that will couple any two of these together so that a second organ can sound at the same time as the one he is playing. The manuals control: the Great organ, which is the most powerful: the Chair, or Choir, a smaller organ sometimes facing the choir and playing for them, and the Swell, another small organ with shutters worked by a foot pedal to rise and fall giving crescendo and diminuendo. The Pedal organ is mainly for playing the bass, but it is possible to play other parts and solo music on it. All have solo voices, and a very large organ will have an extra Solo organ with a fourth manual.

At each side of him are the panels with the stops for each organ; these are pulled out to sound particular ranks of pipes; a rank is a row of pipes from the largest pipe and lowest in pitch to the smallest and highest. There

D

are a number of useful iron composition pedals which bring into play various combinations of stops. The pipes which can be seen by the congregation are the open diapason, the flue pipes of the original organ; they have the special organ tone which when combined with the smaller pipes of the same design is so powerful and thrilling. As well as the open diapason, there are stopped diapason pipes with the tops stoppered or covered to give a different tone, and there are other ranks which can be used singly or in combination.

The other voices fall into three tone families, flute, reed and string tone. The flute group contains the stopped diapason and many others of which the names suggest their tone colours: hohlflote (hollow flute), waldflote (woodland flute), harmonic flute, and gemshorn which sounds like a recorder made from goat's horn.

The next group to be incorporated into organs were the reed pipes. Some, such as hautboy, clarinet or cremona (from krumhorn) suggest these instruments, while others such as trumpet, tuba and bombardon have a tone quality suggesting those; another reed stop is the vox humana, supposedly with the quality of the human voice: "The imitation," says the *Oxford Companion to Music*, "is rather that of a discouraged goat."

The third group are those with string tone: gamba (from the viola da gamba), violone, and others, including aeolina which is supposed to imitate the strains of the aeolian harp.

All these can be enriched and augmented by mutation and mixture stops. Mutation stops sound single ranks of flue pipes sounding at harmonic intervals above the notes played, such as the nazard which sounds an octave and a fifth above it. Mixture stops sound several ranks at once, some, like fourniture, being a powerful mixture, others, like cymbal, brilliant and high pitched, others, such as dulciana mixture, being soft. There is also a tremulant device which causes the note to wobble, a favourite with cinema organists but used with discretion by others.

There are many more stops in each group, many of them bearing the names of instruments. Between about 1850 and 1945 many organists wished to play orchestral music. A moment's reflection, however, will show that since an organist has only two hands and feet, and an orchestra

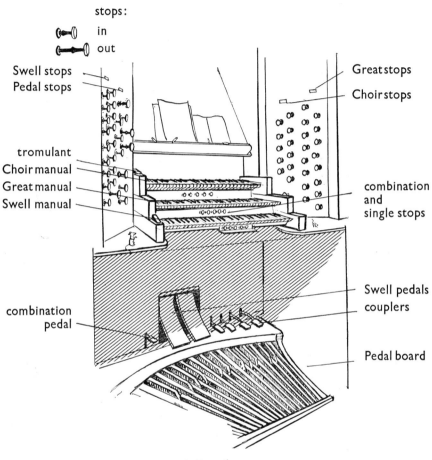

stops:

in

out

Swell stops
Pedal stops

Great stops
Choir stops

tromulant
Choir manual
Great manual
Swell manual

combination
and
single stops

combination
pedal

Swell pedals
couplers

Pedal board

A Console

Some organ pipes

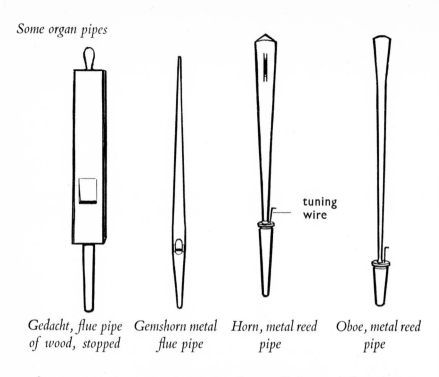

tuning
wire

Gedacht, flue pipe   *Gemshorn metal*   *Horn, metal reed*   *Oboe, metal reed*
of wood, stopped   *flue pipe*   *pipe*   *pipe*

can have twenty-six or more instrumental parts all playing different music, he cannot, even with couplers, imitate the orchestra. Moreover, the players can play *forte* or *piano* as directed, while the organist, except when using the Swell organ, has to increase volume by added ranks of pipes. Organs should play organ music, since organ tone remains organ tone, even though it comes from reed- or string-toned pipes; it is in the interplay of the many voices, the build up or lightening of tone colours, and the use of the component organs in contrast or in combination, that the art of organ playing lies.

Since the tone of the pipes depends on the quality of the wood or metal with which they are made, the shaping of the pipes, and the making and voicing of the various mouths, it follows that the organ builder, who was sometimes an organist as well, has a great deal to do with the sound of the instrument, not only as to the tone, but also as to the variation of voices and the balance of the different groups. This is seen in the national differences in organs in the past, those of France, Italy, Germany, Spain and the Netherlands differing from each other and from those in Britain. The German organs developed the most quickly, and by the time of Bach comprised Great, Positive (Chair) and Pedal; they could play polyphonic music, parts of equal importance interweaving; music for different voices (reed, string, etc.) in harmony; and music with solo parts, the rest accompanying. The British organs at that time had two or three manuals and usually no Pedal, so most of the music of Bach could not be played.

The history of the organ is partly the history of the leading builders, who tended to run in families. As it was among monks and the clergy connected with cathedrals that music was first studied, the first European builders were monks, such as St. Dunstan himself (died 988) who learned to build organs from Irish monks at Glastonbury. These organs consisted of two ranks of flue pipes on a wind chest with a couple of bellowsmen to keep up the air pressure; the pipes were sounded by pulling out a slider, a tongue of wood with holes which then came under the pipes allowing the air to rush in. Organs were spoken of in pairs, like scissors, possibly because these first instruments had a pair of bellows as activators.

However, a few much larger organs were also built in the tenth century, such as the famous Winchester organ; Wulstan's poem about it deserves some quotation:

Early 14th-century Positive, from the Peterborough Psalter. The long R.H. pipe was a drone

Twice six bellows are ranged in a row and fourteen lie below. These by alternate blasts, supply an immense quantity of wind and are worked by seventy strong men, labouring with their arms, covered with perspiration, each inciting his companions to drive the wind up with all his strength that the full-bosomed box may speak with its four hundred pipes . . . Two brethren of concordant spirit sit at the instrument and each manages his own alphabet . . . Like thunder the iron tones batter the ear . . . to such an amount does it reverberate, echoing in every direction, that everyone stops with his hands his gaping ears, being in no wise able to draw near and bear the sound . . .

The alphabet was the keyboard, then consisting of heavy sliders that would make speedy playing impossible. There was another large organ at York,

Some of the twenty bellows of the 14th century organ at Halberstadt. Ten bellows men were employed

*15th-century Portative with press down "typewriter"
keys*

but for the most part the Positive organs which could be played more nimbly were in use. There were dissenting voices, such as Aelred:

> Whence hath the Church so many organs and Musicall Instruments? To what purpose . . . is that terrible noise of blowing of Belloes, expressing rather the crakes of Thunder, than the sweetnesse of a voyce?
>
> *Trans., Prynne, seventeenth century.*

The first known lay builder was Hugh le Organer, working *c.* 1300. Later builders also made clocks, and bells, like John Dyer of Oxford who in 1469 was paid "for mending of the organts and makyng the belyis".

By then, key mechanism had taken the place of the sliders, and a mechanism called tracker action was established; this was simple, the key pulling down and opening a valve, or pallet, which was closed by a spring. Later improvements allowed a type of remote control.

As well as Positives, there were smaller Portatives, little portable organs played by one hand while the other worked the bellows. They were minstrel instruments, and played by minstrels taking part in the Miracle plays, and sometimes in church processions. Landini, the famous blind organist of Florence Cathedral in the fourteenth century, also played a Portative, and "no one had heard such beautiful harmonies, and their hearts almost burst from their bosoms . . ."

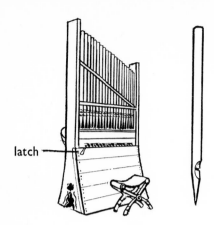

latch

15th-century Flemish Positive. Two rows of pipes with a latch to hold down the lowest note as a drone

Organs alternated with the singers at the Mass, as they still do in Catholic churches abroad. As Chaucer said of Chaunticlere:

> His voys was murier than the murie orgon
> On Messedays that in the churche gon.

A Great or a Positive organ was placed at the west end of the church, and possibly played for festive occasions in the nave as well as for Mass; another organ was placed on the rood screen between chancel and nave; little stairways leading to rood lofts long since pulled down can still be found in some places. It became customary to put a Positive organ near or just behind the organist at the Great organ so that he could play contrasting music; from this it was only a step to incorporating both in one.

Stops came into use in Germany during the fifteenth century, the first being a simple sliding mechanism which cut out ranks from the Blockwerk —the complete pipes of the Great organ. The first known English organ with stops was made by Antony Duddyngton for All Hallows, Barking. His contract specified, among other things, a compass of over three octaves, "Pyppes of fyne metall that is to say of pure Tyn" and "as fewe stops as may be convenient".

The early sixteenth-century Leckingfelde Proverbs dealt with the contemporary organ:

The swete orgayne pipis comfortith a stedfast mynde
Wrong handlynge of the stoppis may cause them sypher fro their kynde.

There was much organ building during the first half of the sixteenth century, including the work of three generations of Howes, the second, John, being known as Father Howe, a term of respect applied to only a few organ builders. Wooden pipes as well as metal were in use here, and there were "grete organ cacez with carven worke". Of that in Durham was written:

> The fairest paire . . . stand over the quire dore (on the rood screen) the pipes beinge of all most fine wood and workmanshipp, very faire, partly gilted upon the inside & outside of the leaves and covers up to the topp with branches and flowers finely gilted with the Name of Jesus painted with gold . . .

With the rise of Puritanism later in the century, organ building for churches slackened because to many its use there was connected with the Church of Rome; it revived under Archbishop Laud in the early seventeenth century. Thomas Dallam was then a noted organ builder, and specifications survive for a two manual organ built in 1613 for Worcester Cathedral; both Great and Chair had five ranks of pipes. This organ was taken down in 1646 when the city was occupied by the Parliamentarians, stored safely, and re-erected at the Restoration. Other organs were saved in this way, including that at Magdalen College, Oxford, which was presented to Cromwell, who had it put up in Hampton Court, where it is said that John Milton played on it. After his death it went back to Oxford and was cared for by Robert Dallam, son of Thomas. The officers of Cromwell's New Model Army often gave instructions that property should be respected; the damage to so many organs was done by the less disciplined and extremist soldiers of the earlier days. So while several very early organs are still to be heard on the continent, none of our Renaissance or pre-Commonwealth organs survive in a fit state to be played, but the body of music composed for them shows that they were capable of interesting music—some of it being "double organ" music, double meaning two manual—and contemporary accounts witness to their sweet voices. Three travellers who made a "Seaven Weekes" Journey round England in 1634 wrote of the "most sweete organ" at Hereford, the "neat, rich and melodious organs" of Bristol, "the sweet sound and richnesse of a fayre organ" at Durham, to name but a few, while Thomas Mace in his book *Musick's Monument* enthusiastically recalls that at York "a most Excellent —large—plump—lusty—full-speaking Organ accompanied choir and congregation in singing a Psalm . . ."

It was a long time before organs came back into the churches; some of the old builders had died or gone abroad during the civil war, and few new men had been trained in what has always been a highly skilled profession.

Robert Dallam returned from France and in the early 1660s submitted a specification for a new organ for New College, Oxford; this comprised Great and Chair, with 24 stops, and in the "forefrant of the organe the bigeste pipe—24 fote long, fittinge for the place & for decorment of the church". This measurement shows the use of a deeper pitched stop than hitherto. The organ also had reed stops. Positive organs called Regals, with very short reed pipes, had been made in the late fifteenth century (see page 80) and some of the first reed stops in organs were called regals. One type of reed stop, called in Germany the Schnarrwerk, had short pipes and a reed tone quality; the other had long cylindrical or slightly conical pipes, and a brass or reed tone quality. There were reed stops in many continental organs in the sixteenth century, but Dallam's is one of the first of which there is any record in England.

Another builder to come home was Bernard Smith. In 1686 Father Smith, as he became known, was paid for building an organ for Durham Cathedral, of which he wrote: "As for the organ I have made for your Catedrall Church, I know it is so good and sound mad as anny in the holl worrelt." He introduced new stops, including the cornet stop used in France and the Low Countries, a powerful solo stop comprising four or five ranks of pipes. In the organ for the Temple Church he introduced the Eccho, a third organ enclosed in a box and useful for faraway effects. He also built the organ, already mentioned on page 49, for the new St. Paul's.

Another was Renatus Harris, grandson of Thomas Dallam, who had grown up in France and brought new ideas from there. Both he and

Late 16th-century case at Framlingham

Bernard Smith were invited to build organs for the Temple Church, one of which would be chosen. There was a "battle of the organs" over this, Harris's friends even cutting the bellows of Smith's organ on the night before the trial between the two. Although the voicing of Harris's reeds was superior, Smith won the contract after four years of deliberation, and his work set the pattern for British organ building for over a century to come. Father Smith built many fine organs, and pipework of some is still in use.

Case by Renatus Harris, in St. James's Piccadilly, 1686–1688. The smaller Chaire or Choir case was added in 1852

Father Smith's work was carried on by his son-in-law, Christopher Shrider, and Harris's by his son and his son-in-law John Byfield, whose descendants continued the profession until after 1800. In 1726, two years after his father's death, John Harris built an organ at St. Mary Redcliffe, Bristol, with Great, Chair, Swell, and Pedal governing thirteen notes. The Swell was first made in 1712 by the Abraham Jordans; it was a device on an Eccho organ, at first a single shutter that was pulled up and down by a string attached to a pedal to increase and decrease the sound; this "Nag's head" shutter gave way later to a slatted shutter like a Venetian blind. At about the same time Shrider added pedals to the organ at St. Paul's, as well as "the Loudning & Softning . . . the Swelling Note & its Movments & other things thereto belonging".

The England family was among those trained in the Harris tradition, and continued organ building into the nineteenth century, when one of their workmen was to found the still flourishing firm of J. J. Walker and Sons. Another of many builders was Johann Snetzler, who came from the Swiss–German border; his chamber organs, of which some survive, were particularly fine, and much of his pipe work remains in Beverley Minster. It is recorded how he disapproved of a certain organist and ran about the church crying out: "Te tevil, te tevil, he run over te key like one cat; he vill not give my pipes room for to shpeak."

The organs of this period were beautifully voiced as well as beautifully cased, and in a way peculiar to this country. The authors of *The British Organ* speak of the robust solo reed stops and the brilliance and vitality of the smaller pipes—the upperwork. The pedals governed only a row of wooden pipes lightly blown and used for holding bass notes, and the instruments could not play music composed for continental organs with more developed pedal work. Nevertheless, the instrument was extremely popular where it could be heard in the larger churches and chapels. The Surrey Chapel in London used to hold audiences of 2,000 to hear the organists Samuel Wesley and Benjamin Jacob give long recitals on such an organ.

Early in the nineteenth century efforts were made to develop organ building, but it was not until 1841 and the building of the organ in George

Street Chapel, Liverpool, that success was achieved. This organ had fifty-two speaking stops—"speaking" as opposed to devices such as couplers—including six stops on the Pedal organ, and a solo heavy pressure stop, the tuba mirabilis. The Swell was developed with more powerful mixtures and reed stops, so that it became second in importance to the Great, leaving the Chair for some solo, and for accompaniment. This organ, which could play many sorts of organ music, was the work of William Hill and Dr. Henry Gauntlett, a brilliant organist who started his career as church organist at the age of nine. Many of the organs they built have been "improved", but fortunately for music lovers in Northern Ireland, that at the Ulster Hall remains to show how fine they were. (At this period, civic pride and increased wealth led to many towns buying big concert organs for public performances.)

The work of Hill and Gauntlett was followed by other builders, not all so successful. Nor were all organists successful in managing the stops and devices, which seem to have gone to their heads. Sir John Sutton, who wrote in 1847 a comprehensive Short Account of Organs built in England, explained this and the destruction of many of the older organs thus:

> The clergy and those in authority are persuaded that the instruments are not fit to play upon; by which they mean that it is impossible to show off upon them in the most approved fashion, for they have neither pedals, swells, or any of those complicated contrivances with which these modern Music Mills are crowded . . . In the chanting of the Psalms, the attention is continually drawn from the voices by the perpetual changing of stops and the clattering of the composition pedals, for the modern Cathedral Organist scarcely ever accompanies six verses on the same stops, or even the same row of keys, and keeps up a continual thundering with the pedals . . . when perhaps the choir he is accompanying consists of ten little boys and six or at most ten men, three or four of whom are either disabled by old age, or a long continued habit of drunkenness . . .

Not a cheerful picture of some cathedral music! The singing was probably much more enthusiastic in parish churches with the musickers, and in chapels, especially in Wales, and in Scotland where, for the first time since the Reformation, organs were allowed into some churches.

Barrel organ c. 1805

In some churches there were barrel organs. These were pipe organs mechanically played by inserting a barrel, or a rotating metal cylinder, with pins that set off the mechanism to sound the pipes. Very small mechanical organs were put in clocks to play a tune at the hour; Thomas Dallam had made one as early as 1598, with the addition of chimes, and clockwork trumpeters and singing birds. The larger chamber and church organs, however, needed someone to turn the handle. They were popular in the eighteenth century, and could be used not only for entertainment but devotion in the home, as one could have a collection of barrels that played religious music. They were introduced into parish churches to replace the band. There are stories of abrupt cessations of the music, explained as "the 'anell" being stuck, or in one case by a mouse in the works, while some would not stop playing, one reputed to have continued even when buried. One still remains in the parish church at Brightling, Sussex.

Among organ builders showing work at the Great Exhibition were the French builder Cavaillé-Coll, whose organs were suited only to romantic music calling for power and expression, and Schulze from Germany whose work was to influence ("bedevil" is Clutton's word) British organ building for the next hundred years by adding power to the diapasons. There was also a young English builder, Henry Willis, who obtained a commission to build an organ for St. George's Hall in Liverpool, which was a completely modern organ—apart from the absence of electricity—with pneumatic lever action to sound the pipes, heavy pressure for some ranks, a modern console, and a radiating pedal board of which a distinguished but disapproving organist stated: "My dear sir, I never in my life played on a gridiron!" Henry Willis became know as Father Willis and founded the firm bearing his name; Father Willis pipework can be found in many churches.

By the end of the century, most parish churches had an organ installed, and the musickers were disbanded:

> Having nothing to do with conducting the service for almost the first time in their lives, they all felt awkward, out of place, abashed, and inconvenienced by their hands . . . The venerable body of musicians could not help thinking that the simpler notes they had been wont to bring forth were more in keeping with the simplicity of their old church than the crowded chords and intervals it was her (the organist's) pleasure to produce.
>
> *From a description of the first service with the organ; Thomas Hardy, "Under the Greenwood Tree".*

Hardy is right about simplicity; had the organ been more simple, and played with the band instead of displacing it by its plenitude of tone colours and volume, then both might have progressed together on the path of religious music, and the country people have felt themselves still part of their services, instead of a gradually dwindling audience. On the other hand, the new organists took their calling seriously, and trained choirs of local people.

It would be a fair analogy to compare the best nineteenth-century organs

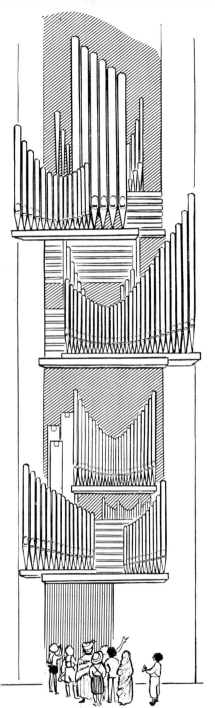

and those of the Renaissance with a painting by Turner and an Elizabethan miniature: the latter has a limited range of colours, some bright, some soft, some deeper in tone, and all harmonious and clearly delineated one from the other; the former has a wide range of colours, some fiery and dramatic, others cool and silvery, some clear and bright, others gloomy and dark, and the colours are often so glazed or scumbled or cross-hatched one over the other that it is only by looking closely that one can distinguish the many layers of paint that make up the picture. Turner could work magic, while some people couldn't be trusted with a paint-box; this sort of thing sometimes happened with organ building and playing: at the end of the century an electrical engineer, Hope-Jones, built organs, producing unusual sounds from exaggerated pipe and mouth shapes; these could not play any organ music already written, and only one important piece was composed for them, but they had a bad effect on the voicing of many British organs, and much harm was

65

Case in Jesus College Chapel, Cambridge, by Pugin, a founder of the Victorian Gothic style

done to the pipework of many old and beautiful instruments in an effort to obtain these new tone colours. Fortunately, good organs were built by the firm of Harrison; Arthur Harrison worked in collaboration with Colonel Dixon, a north country musician who had known Father Willis. In this tradition, Henry, grandson of Father Willis, built two magnificent organs in the 1920s, in the Liverpool and Westminster Cathedrals.

At present there is a return to the classical organ, with the influence of the eighteenth-century German instruments. Electrical actions still linger on, but more and more organists favour a return to, and all the better builders now build, tracker action. A pleasant innovation is the unencased organ, in which much of the hitherto hidden pipework is open to view; this is especially effective in Coventry Cathedral, where the organ pipes make a dramatic contribution to the appearance of the nave.

This brief survey leaves many things to further study by the questioning student, such as the development of the various mechanisms, for instance the bellows: when electric pumps were fitted in Winchester Cathedral, they did not displace seventy bellowsmen! Then there are the names, tone-colours and roles of the stops, the way the pipes are constructed, and their tuning, which is a technical matter unlike that of any other instrument; the design and workmanship of the cases; the music composed for organs during the different epochs of their history; and so on. Such students are referred to the list of books by experts on page 120. My usual advice to interested students is "play it", but this is not so easy with the organ, since few are privileged to learn this instrument. However, there is ample opportunity to listen. Not only are there broadcasts and recordings of many famous and historic organs, but almost everyone can listen "live" in places of worship; there are six organs within a mile of my home, one with Father Willis pipework. The authors of *The British Organ* append a list of interesting organs to be heard and seen in all localities; the interested student, listening critically yet appreciatively to one organ after another, and, with permission, examining the casing and installation, may be rewarded by finding some gem of the organ builder's art still being played without fuss and vanity, an instrument in the service of its congregation's faith.

4

ALTHOUGH STRINGED INSTRUMENTS of orchestra and pop music are now heard in church for special performances, they have had no part in everyday church music since the break-up of the church bands. Guitars supporting voices have became part of Salvation Army music, and in the early days of the Army there were string as well as brass bands. In 1890 there was a Festival of Music held at the Crystal Palace with not only "a battle of song" but performances of massed string bands as well as massed brass, and at many a pioneer Salvation meeting the violin was played to accompany the singing. The most famous of these violinists was Captain Eliza Haynes, called Happy Eliza because of her success in attracting people to the meetings by rushing through the streets of Nottingham with a banner saying "Happy Eliza" streaming from her hair. Later, violin in hand and beating time with the bow, she led a procession of converted ruffians through the same streets; entirely fearless, she was next sent to London, and campaigned in the Edgware Road sitting in front of a cab playing her violin and calling to the people to be saved; on top of the cab was her drummer, Welsh Tom. She became a famous figure of her time.

Strings were part of nearly all the church bands (see page 26); the fiddle was a folk instrument, played for dancing and merrymaking, so there were fiddlers in most villages, and they took their place in the band. When Thomas Hardy was young, there were still a few church bands left in Dorset, and he had doubtless heard the old musickers talk as they talk in *Under the Greenwood Tree*. Apart from a romance, this is the story of how such a band was supplanted, with the best of intentions of an earnest young vicar, by a new organ. They discuss their instruments, and while one says "There's always a rakish, scampish countenance about a fiddle that seems to say that the Wicked One had a hand in makin o'en" they are agreed

Happy Eliza in the Edgware Road (from a contemporary drawing)

that "nothing will speak to your heart wi' the sweetness of the man of strings". Theirs was an entirely string band, three fiddles and a 'cello; slightly earlier bands are listed with woodwind and the bass viol. On one occasion the rector took a part in the band, the old sexton of Burwash in Sussex describing how "he had a hem o' trouble with the boys (choristers) and the only way he could make 'em behave reasonable like was to crack 'em on the head with his fiddlestick. He was old-fashioned no bounds, was the Rector."

The bass viol was often a 'cello, sometimes made by the musician himself; I have seen a metal cello which was made and played by the village blacksmith. The double bass, called a Grandmother Fiddle, was also found at times. The bass viol was also the old viola de gamba (see page 29) the bass member of the viol family, which lingered on in use when the rest of the viols had become obsolete; it was the only instrument which John and Charles Wesley would allow into the first Methodist meetings.

Folk Fiddler

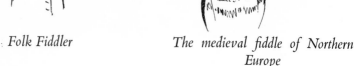

The medieval fiddle of Northern
Europe

The violin had come into the musical world after the Restoration,
Charles II bringing back with him an orchestra of twenty-four violins
(which included violas and violincellos) some of which, as we have seen,
he ordered to play in the music of the Chapel Royal. Some of the music
composed at that time for performance during the service used the
orchestra; strings, woodwind, trumpets, drums, and in church the organ
instead of harpsichord; it is doubtful if such an ensemble were heard outside a few large cities.

On the continent there was a richer tradition of instrumental playing
in cathedrals, especially in the south. An English traveller to Venice wrote
in 1608 of seeing in St. Mark's: "Ten sagbuts, foure Cornets, and two
Viol de Gambas . . . and sometimes two singular fellowes played together
upon Theorboes." (Theorboes were long-necked lutes with extra strings.)
Sixteenth-century Spanish cathedrals had full-time musicians playing
shawms, cornets, flutes, sackbuts, organ and harp.

During the English Renaissance, there is little evidence of instruments
other than the organ being played in church, outside the Chapel Royal
and a few large cathedrals. The viol (see page 22) may have been used to
support or take vocal parts in polyphony, its gentle sound blending well
with voices. It had six strings, and a fretted fingerboard, and was always

70

The Rebec

played resting on the knee, with the bow held palm upwards. New and surviving viols can be heard today played by those musicians who specialize in music and instruments of the past.

Medieval fiddles were played during religious processions and at Mysteries. The medieval fiddle took various forms, but most in this country were like the north European Minnesinger fiddle, a four-stringed, slightly waisted instrument tuned in various ways and lower in pitch than the modern fiddle.

A medieval instrument often played with the fiddle, and also portrayed in the hands of angels as well as minstrels, was the rebec, a pear-shaped instrument coming from the Near East in the eleventh century; this usually had three strings, and a sturdy soundbox carved from a single block of wood, with a raised fingerboard. Later it became a folk instrument, associated like the bagpipes with dancing, and probably played at rituals of the Old Faith.

Another instrument sometimes shaped as a fiddle started as a church instrument (see page 13), although when the organ added more voices it became first a minstrel's instrument and finally a folk instrument. This was the organistrum, later called symphony, and later still hurdy gurdy. It is not until the twelfth century that we find it portrayed in carvings or MSS.;

The organistrum (in the 12th-century the tangents were operated by hand turned rods

it was then about five feet long, with one player to turn the handle of the wheel that sounded the strings, and another to work the stopping mechanism for different notes. There were two mechanisms, the earlier with tangents coming up to touch the string as a rod was turned, and the more usual later tangents pressed against the string by keys; some early stringed instruments were played with the back of the fingernail pressed against the string in the same way. The organistrum was very useful in churches and monasteries as its strings could be tuned to accord with the musical intervals of the chant and early polyphony of the time. It was a development of the monochord, an instrument used in monasteries for musical experiment and research; this had one string stretched over a soundbox,

The monochord

Tromba Marina, 17th-century

and a series of movable bridges which could be used to determine the exact interval between the notes of the scales. Many treatises were written about it, one by an Irish scholar in 867; a thirteenth-century scholar wrote: "Man sings to the best of his ability, but the string is divided by scholars with such skill that it cannot lie."

The monochord had another offspring, also apparently played in church at some time. It was a three-sided tapering soundbox with a single string, plucked by the player. By the fifteenth century this had been elaborated into an instrument with one or two strings bowed above the fingers which lightly touched, not pressed, the strings, thus causing the bow to sound harmonic notes only, high, clear, penetrating sounds. It was played for some church music in France. Later a bridge was added which had one leg fixed to lead the string vibrations to the soundbox as does the bridge of any stringed instrument, and the other slightly longer leg left free so that it drummed on the soundbox; the German name was Trumscheit, or drum log. The effect of the drumming and the harmonic notes gave it a trumpet-like sound, and it came to this country in the seventeenth century as the tromba marina, or marine trumpet. It seems to have been a musical curiosity rather than anything else, and all sorts of reasons were advanced for its name. It was also called the Nun's fiddle, on account of an idea that nuns used it to play trumpet music in convents.

Other instruments mentioned and portrayed in early MSS. are psaltery, harp, crwth and rotta, sometimes called rote. King David is sometimes drawn playing the rotta, which was a lyre found in northern Europe and Scandinavia. In its later form it had as many as seventeen strings, and was still played as a plucked instrument after the tenth century, gradually giving way to the bowed lyres of northern Europe. It is possible that the harp so dear to the Saxons, and mentioned in their poetry, and called the joywood, was in fact a rotta. There is much confusion as to the names and translations of names of early stringed instruments. Several rottas have been found in Saxon burial places; in one grave a German warrior was found with his sword and bow beside him and his rotta clasped in his arms.

The only bowed lyre found in the British Isles is the Welsh crwth. This was one of the Bardic instruments, harp, pipes and crwth, and in its early days must have been a rotta-like lyre since there is no record of bowed instruments here before the eleventh century; crwth players were of two classes, one associated with bardic music, and the other, who played a three-stringed crwth, with revelry and dance and who were often accused of furthering the work of the devil. As a bowed instrument it was also played in England, since it appears in carvings in English churches although much less frequently than the fiddle and rebec. Like them, it was a min-

Saxon rotta or rote

strel instrument which later fell into the hands of folk players when the minstrels developed other instruments. It continued to be played in Wales until the end of the eighteenth century, and perhaps longer in some places; however, very few Welsh crwths are known to survive; possibly they did not find favour with the Methodist movement because of their pagan connections. In its surviving form the crwth has two bourdon strings in addition to the melody strings, which could be bowed, or plucked with the left thumb. The bridge has one foot resting on the soundboard as in other instruments, and the other goes through the soundhole carrying the vibrations to the back of the instrument.

The Welsh harp, the telyn (see page 34), survived Methodism, and was allowed to play in chapel; after all, David played the harp, so all Christians believed, which sanctified even an instrument which had been for so long the chief of the Bardic instruments, the one which the bards themselves played, and which, so legend has it, could so assuage the passions of men so that opposing armies would make peace with each other. It had been moreover, an essential to all Welshmen, and to own and play it was the mark of a freeman, since no slave was allowed a harp. The present-day triple harp is thought to have been taken over from a similar seventeenth-century Italian instrument; it has three rows of strings, a diatonic scale on the outer rows, with the sharps and flats in the inner; it is extremely hard to play, and the art has almost died out. However, the shape of the harp is similar to that of the older telyn, with a straight forepillar, although the telyn had a single row of strings; in early

Irish harp, 14th or 15th century   *Medieval English harp, the "Cythara Anglica"*

medieval times these were of horse hair, and the Welsh despised the Irish harp with its metal strings and louder tone.

The Irish harp also has a long Bardic tradition. The bards of ancient Ireland were second only to the king in rank (the king could wear seven colours in his dress, the bards six). The highest order of bards were the poets and heralds who marched ahead of their armies in war; these themselves played the harp. Those who were solely instrumentalists were the fourth order. These old harps, to judge from carvings on Celtic crosses, were quadrilateral in appearance; no details remain in these carvings, but similarly shaped harps appear in later carvings in churches on the continent; they may have been brought to Europe by Irish harpers who have always been famous and much in demand abroad, or have some common ancestor in the harps of the East. The well-known clarsach, the harp of Ireland, developed later, the earliest suviving one being the thirteenth-century harp in Trinity College Dublin; this was a sturdy instrument, the soundbox carved from a single block of wood, and played in the old way with the fingernails which were allowed to grow very long.

At the same time, the harp was so popular in England that the instrument rather similar to the clarsach, was called the English harp. No knight or lord was without a harper, and this included the princes of the Church;

although there is no evidence of a harp being played during worship, its music inspired at least one bishop, the famous Robert Grosseteste of Lincoln, to write:

> The vertu of the harpe thrughe skylle and ryght
> Will destroy the fendes (fiend's) myght:
> And to the croys (Cross)by god skylle
> Is the harpe lyhered weyle.

This attributes to the harp the power against evil that it had in the hands of pre-Christian Welsh and Irish bards, powers shared in the Church only by the bells.

Harp and psaltery are often mentioned together in the writings of the early Church as they were thought to have been of Biblical origin; new light has been thrown on the Biblical instruments (see Chapter 10) and the psaltery, like so many instruments later played in the West, appears to have been of Eastern origin. A square ten-stringed instrument is mentioned and illustrated by St. Jerome c. A.D. 340–420, and a similar square psaltery with only four strings appears in an eleventh-century Spanish carving. Later psalteries had soundboxes of various shapes, triangular, wingshaped, some like a pig's head—called in Italy Strumento do Porco—and many like a triangle with the top cut off. The strings were plucked with quills, and at some time players used beaters and the instrument was called a dulcimer; in the northern parts of Europe it was used as a dulcimer, in the south as a psaltery and can be found in both forms as a folk instrument. In the Middle Ages it was a minstrel instrument, and only played in churches for processions and mysteries, although because of its Biblical connections it is often portrayed in the hands of angels.

Early medieval four stringed psaltery
(see also half-title)

Church band with viola da gamba, bassoon, two clarinets and oboe

5

THE REED INSTRUMENTS are wind pipes in which the sound is made by the vibrations of either a single reed against an aperture cut in a tube, such as the clarinet reed, or of a double reed, two reeds vibrating against each other, such as the oboe reed. In most cases, the reeds vibrate inside the mouth, and can be tongued, that is, touched with the tongue, to separate the notes.

Clarinet, oboe and bassoon were played in the church bands, not in their modern orchestral form with their present systems of keys and fingering.

The clarinet was usually the old five- or six-keyed instrument, made of boxwood, and with the reed tied in place. This instrument had been developed by Johann Denner, an instrument maker of Nuremburg; it had a cylindrical bore, and eight fingerholes, the top one being keyed, and two thumb holes at the back, one keyed. This gave it the upward range of notes with the high "clarino" trumpet-like quality which gave it its name. Later, as in other woodwind instruments, more keys were added to increase the downward range and to facilitate the playing of certain passages.

It was very popular in church bands, in spite of the advice given by one of Hardy's musickers (*Under the Greenwood Tree*). "Depend upon't, if so be you have them tooting clar'nets, you'll spoil the whole set-out. Clar'nets were not made for the service of Providence; you see it by looking at 'em." Jane Carlyle, wife of the eminent historian Thomas Carlyle, would have agreed: when she went to a country church in Suffolk she heard "a shrill clear sound, something between a squeal of agony and the highest tone of a bagpipe" which she was informed was "a clarionet."

One of the old musicianers of Sussex related how his grandfather, who played the clarinet behind him in his place as a choirboy, "would, if he stopped singing for a moment, thrust the bell of his clarionet into the lad's ear, and blow a shrill and mighty blast to urge him to renewed effort". One clarinettist became famous for his music, and is depicted by a contemporary artist in 1850 playing the anthem "Awake, thou that sleepest" in order to wake up the congregation.

Reed instruments frequently played in Church bands

Bassoon c. 1800, rear view showing thumb holes and keys

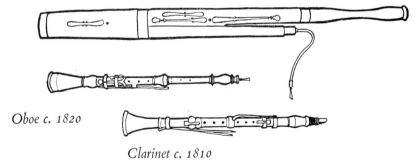

Oboe c. 1820

Clarinet c. 1810

The oboe, in an early form with two or three keys, and known in Dorset as the vox humaner, was played less often. The oboe developed from the medieval shawm, a rough loud instrument with a conical bore, at one time used in battle; the improved oboe, or French hautbois, as it was then known, was introduced here after the Restoration in 1660, and has since been refined and given systems of keys and fingering.

More popular was the bassoon, one of the instruments that was developed from the bass shawm; this had been up to eight feet long, and was very awkward for the processional music for which it was chiefly played, so experiments were made with folded bass instruments, of which the bassoon, or fagot because it resembled a bundle of sticks, alone remains, and has become an important bass voice in the orchestra and military band. The bassoon of the church bands was the old four- to six-keyed instrument, known to the players as "the horse's leg". As it is not easy to play, its frequent use pays tribute to the perseverance and ability of the village musicians. The note is deep and rich, but it can be made to bray like a donkey. In the 1890s a local MP gave the church band of Brightling, in Sussex, nine bassoons in order to drown the voices of the choir. At the same period, the band at West Tarring, Sussex, had "base-viols, bassoons, hautbois and flutes" and "was not spoken of in very flattering terms by the old inhabitants . . . although it seems to have given satisfaction to the performers themselves" (from *Transcripts and Records of the Past*, E. Sayers).

Three distinguished musicians of the seventeenth and early eighteenth century, Henry Purcell, Dr. John Blow, and Father Smith, had held the official appointment which gave them the care of "the King's Regalls, Virginalls, and Organs". The regal was by then out of date, although it had been very popular, especially with Henry VIII, who had eighteen in his various palaces. It was a small organ, invented about 1460, with reed instead of flue pipes. The reeds were made of metal, but beat against an aperture like that of the clarinet, and unlike those of the later harmonium (see Chapter 7). This gave it a different sound from the flue pipe organs, and quite a small reed pipe could make a deeper and more powerful sound than a whistle pipe of the same size. Regals were often made as portatives, and in the sixteenth century George Voll of Nuremburg made one which

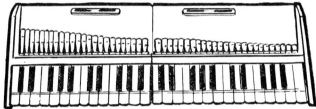

Section showing the reeds

could be closed up like a book; these Bible regals were used in Germany into the last century to accompany village church choirs. Earlier regals were used to accompany choirs in the plainsong, and sometimes played with the main organ; St. Martin-in-the-Fields, for instance, had "small regalls" in 1560. They were also played in church processions and mystery plays.

Regal was the name given to the first reed stops incorporated into the organ, and regal organs often had flue pipes as well, as their lists of stops makes evident: one of Henry VIII's had "one stopp of Tinne, one Regalle of tinne, and a Cimball"; the last-named was a rank or ranks of brilliant toned flue pipes.

In many parts of Europe, single reeds have been fitted into pipes of bone or wood with six finger holes, and a horn at the end for a bell. Sometimes another section of horn was fitted over the reed, which was not taken into the mouth. In Scotland this instrument was called a stockhorn, and in Wales a pibcorn. Pibcorns were played in Wales as late as the eighteenth century, and may have been the pipes of which Giraldus Cambrensis, Bishop of Wales, wrote in the twelfth century.

Bagpipes were reed pipes tied into a bag to give a reservoir of air which would allow for continuous playing. They were both minstrel and folk instruments from the twelfth century onwards, until they became relegated to folk music during the reign of Elizabeth. As such, they were played at the dances and ceremonies of the Old Religion. In Scotland and Ireland, however, they had always been war pipes, the *piob mor* or Great pipes, and continued as such to the present day, possessing like their ancestors the loud shawms of the armies of Eastern potentates the power to spur on their own men and to scare the daylights out of the other side; as

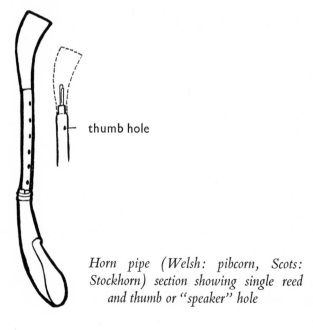

thumb hole

Horn pipe (Welsh: pibcorn, Scots: Stockhorn) section showing single reed and thumb or "speaker" hole

16th-century Irish war pipes

with the shawms, the bagpipes were always in the thick of the battle, again a tradition that has lasted to the present day. They illustrate very clearly the power of a certain type of instrumental music over human emotions and help one understand how in earlier times an instrument could be thought to be possessed by supernatural power.

The war pipes have a double reed chanter or melody pipe, with three drones, tuned one bass—two octaves below the keynote, and two tenor, one octave below; the Irish pipes have one of the tenor drones tuned at a fifth below. There used to be smaller pipes in Scotland, played for singing and dancing as in England; the folk pipes of Ireland differ in being bellows blown, and have become with the introduction of two keyed drones as well as two others, a more complicated instrument.

The ancestors of the reed instruments are the pipes of herdsmen and shepherds, made as little boys used to make them from green corn, with a tongue cut beneath a notch, or from a stem folded and slit to make a double reed. It is likely that these pipes were played at rituals and festivities connected with the Old Faith. One certainly connected with magic was the Whithorn, made of coiled willow bark fastened together with the thorns of the blackthorn, and with a double reed made from a tube of bark; similar horns are made in other parts of Europe. In the last century country boys still made Whithorns and May whistles, and went round the villages playing them to call the people to the old festival of Beltane that preceded Whitsun. Beltane, or Bel-tein, was one of the European May festivals, and was celebrated in Wales, Ireland and Scotland as late as the nineteenth century. The Beltane fires were lit, and a sacrificial victim had to jump through the flames. In much earlier times he had perished in the fire as a real sacrifice to some long ago fertility god, and the sound of the Whithorn had a more sinister magic.

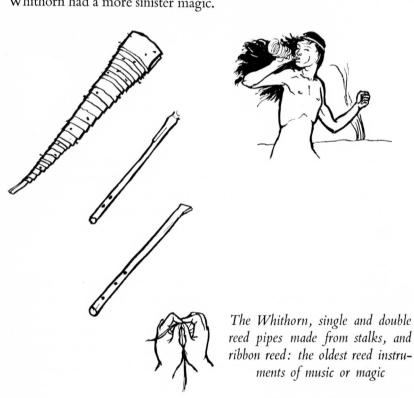

The Whithorn, single and double reed pipes made from stalks, and ribbon reed: the oldest reed instruments of music or magic

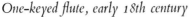
One-keyed flute, early 18th century

6   FLUTES AND WHISTLE PIPES

IN THESE INSTRUMENTS the sound-making vibrations are caused by a flat jet of air striking a straight edge; this is called edge tone. In transverse or cross flutes the air is directed from the player's mouth against the side of the mouth-hole; in fipple or block flutes, such as recorders, it is directed through a slit in the mouthpiece to the sound-hole in the pipe. In end-blown flutes, such as panpipes, the air is again directed straight from the player's mouth across the top of the pipe.

The cross flute, which now has a complicated key and fingering mechanism, was a popular instrument with church musicianers; it had then one key only to give an extra note at the bottom of its range, and was often made of boxwood. As well as providing a descant voice in the band, it could be used to give the note, and as the Rev. MacDermott remarks: "as a rod for the castigation of small choir-boys". (Incidentally, girls were often preferred as choristers because they behaved better.) An old in-habitant wrote at the turn of the century about "the old Choir at Climping where we lived so many years and generations before us ... the Blacksmith and his Son playing the Violins and the Churchwarden the Bass Viol and

85

two others the Shoemakers play'd a Flute each they all wore White Smock Frocks and carried their instruments and manuscript music in a Red Handkerchief. . . ." A good picture, complete with the white Sunday smocks and the hand-copied music; and a good balance of instruments.

With the direct control of the player and the sweet high tones of the flute itself, it is possible to play it with much feeling. In parts of Italy, it was not long ago forbidden the young men to serenade with the flute, on account of its powers of seduction. During the nineteenth and eighteenth centuries it was a romantic instrument much played by gentlemen, while their ladies favoured the harp and piano, an interesting echo of the part played by flutes and stringed instruments in masculine and feminine rituals among primitive peoples. The flute has been from earliest times mainly played by men; it was much associated with courtship and love songs, again an echo of its part in fertility rituals. Flute players were condemned by one of the Puritan pamphleteers as "caterpillars of the Commonwealth", and also by the early Christian fathers on account of their part in pagan worship.

The cross flute is still part of the folk culture of the Balkans; it did not come to England until after the Renaissance, so the folk flute of this country is the whistle, and, in its early days, the recorder. The medieval recorder was made in one piece, with a wide bore, and sounded shrill, hence its name from Old English "record": to sing like a bird; it was played for dancing so may well have been played for dances of the Old

Medieval recorder

Descant recorder from Praetorius (1619). It has a speaker hole for the thumb

Playing position of hand

Pipe and tabor, from an early 14th century MS

Religion as well as other merrymaking. The whistle pipes played by present-day folk musicians are like those made by workmen in the early industrial era, the tin whistles, and which were previously made from wood or bone; they have a long association with the Old Religion, and the earliest known here is a bone pipe found in an Iron Age burial mound in Yorkshire.

The three-holed pipe played in conjunction with a drum, the tabor, is the traditional music for many old folk dances of Europe. Here they were used to accompany the Whitsun Morris dances, and every district had its own player. The pipe has a narrow bore which makes it easy to play high harmonics by overblowing, so that with only three holes, two at the front and one behind, he can play a scale; each finger position gives from one to four harmonic notes. The ring dances are descended from the ring rituals of the Old Religion; a Paleolithic cave painting in Spain shows women dancing round a male figure. One of the simplest whistle pipes is the one-note May whistle made from willow, and played with the Whithorn (see page 84) to arouse the country people for the spring festival.

The panpipes, as their name denote, were associated with the old Greek

Panpipes used to give correct pitch for church singing

country god, Pan, a horned god who was worshipped in Greece long before the coming of Zeus or Apollo. They were made in two ways, either a graduated row of canes or wooden pipes bound together, with the lower ends stopped, or a block of wood or pottery with the graduated holes drilled or made in; some are endblown, and some are duct pipes, that is having mouthpieces like whistle pipes. They are still a folk instrument in some parts of Europe. An eleventh-century MS. shows David as a shepherd boy playing panpipes, so they were evidently a rustic instrument in the early Middle Ages; later they appear as a minstrel instrument as well, sometimes in a rounded form, the pipes set in a circle; they have been played in church during the twelfth century as they appear among the sacred music on page 17. All these pipes go back into the mists of time, and some were connected with gods.

A whistle of practical religious use during the last three centuries or so is the pitch pipe, or spoke pipe as it was called in Sussex churches. This is a whistle with the piston at the end with the notes of the scale marked on it which was pulled out to the appropriate note for each vocal part of the hymn or psalm. It was in the hands of the parish clerk, and although it could give the note for tuning the instruments, it was more often used when there was no accompanying music at all, such as little churches or chapels where there was no band, barrel organ or harmonium. One Sussex musicianer recalls how in 1848, at the age of ten, he had to give the singers the note with the pitch pipe as well as play the violin, the other players being the schoolmaster with the bass viol, the vicar's gardener

88

with the clarinet, and the head gardener of a local lady with the flute . . .
"but the plug of the pipe sometimes got pushed in just before I blew it,
and I shall never forget the discordant noise, nor, to me, the awful sounds
usually produced by the instruments".

Pitch pipes were used in the chapels and meeting houses of the early
Wesleyans, and the dissenting sects of the Restoration period, and in
churches during the Commonwealth. This was before any musical instrument was admitted to their services. Singing, especially psalmody, was
the important act of worship, but even the most extreme dissenter needed
a note for his singing, and that the pitch pipe provided, although how long
the singers kept up the pitch history does not say.

Pitchpipe

The Angel Adjutant

7

THE FREE REED is a metal tongue that vibrates through an aperture when wind is applied, the pitch being determined by the length and weight of the tongue. Free reeds do not need a large windchamber in which to vibrate, as witness the harmonica, and they can make a loud noise with something of organ quality. The concertina was patented in 1844 by its maker Sir Charles Wheatstone, and although not the first European free reed instrument, it soon became the most popular of its time, and was well established in the world of folk and popular music by the time the Salvation Army took it up. Not only could it augment a small band, but it could accompany hymns alone, even at an outdoor meeting; moreover it was light, and easier to play than a brass instrument, and could be managed by Salvationists frail in body if strong in spirit.

One of the early Army players was summonsed in 1887 for playing in the streets "an instrument not strictly known to the musical world, and called a concertina". (The magistrates were somewhat behind the times.) Another was a young woman known as the Angel Adjutant. At that time there were pubs and dives in London into which the police dared not go, even in couples; the Angel Adjutant, however, accompanied only by her concertina, went unhesitatingly into these places, which could be accurately described as "dens of vice", and there sang hymns and called souls to salvation, often with success.

The earliest European free reed instruments were organs, such as the *orgue expressif* made in Paris in 1810, and the bellows harmonica made in Vienna in 1818. These had keyboards and were worked with foot pedals; other small reed organs had a small manual played by one hand, while the other worked the bellows. Various types were made, useful for playing at home, especially for family hymn singing. In 1848 the harmonium appeared, made by Debain of Paris, with a single foot pedal, and two sets of reeds, the second set tuned a little out with the first so as to give a tremulant when the stop was drawn; in addition, it had an expression stop, which worked a valve to bypass the windchest where pressure was equalized as in the pipe organ, and so apply wind pressure direct to the reeds for *piano* and *forte*. Other makers built harmoniums, Andre and Mustel being the chief in Paris; Mustel's instruments are regarded as the

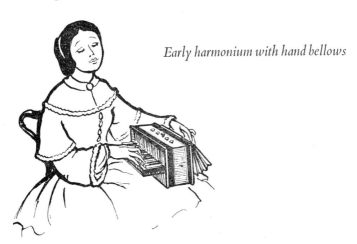

Early harmonium with hand bellows

Evans New English Harmonium 1859

best in tone and workmanship. Stops were added, named like organ stops, controlling sets of reeds of differing length and weight and size of wind-chamber—those with the smaller windchambers gave a louder note, such as the trumpet and tuba stops. In England, Evans built the New English Harmonium in 1859; it had two five-octave manuals, the upper with six stops and the lower with ten, and a two and a half octave pedal board; the bellows were foot-operated, and the swell device was worked by pushing two carved doors outward with the knees, so the player needed to be athletic as regards the legs. A harmonium made in America used suction instead of windpressure.

There was a great demand for harmoniums, from the New English, which was powerful enough for a church and, to the untutored ear, "as good as a real organ", to the little folding models that could be taken to indoor or outdoor mission meetings. There were various sects with little meeting houses and chapels tucked away in humble streets, there were the many chapels of Methodists and Baptists, and there was the increasing mission activity of the Church of England, with meetings and Bible classes in church halls. Here was a useful adaptable instrument, with enough of organ tone to sound religious, with no pipes to take up the space, easy to play and keep in tune, and not expensive; as an advertisement of 1859 puts it: "It is a little band in itself . . . The Vicar's lady or the family governess, by the aid of a small guide book and a few days' practice, will become competent to accompany psalms and chants." This was true, and very piously romantic it was for Victorian and Edwardian ladies to play while little white-surpliced choir boys sang in the choir stalls, but, as the Rev. MacDermott says: "With the arrival of the organ, the harmonium and its feeble sister the American organ, all the old musicianers and lusty singers, with their boundless enthusiasm and fervent diligence, their homely piety and simple sincerity, disappeared from our churches, perhaps for ever."

The first makers of these instruments got the idea from the mouth organs of the Far East which have been played for over 3,000 years, instruments in which free reeds sounded in pipes of differing length, giving a lovely sound. Another even more ancient free reed instrument is the Jews' harp or guimbard, in which a slender metal reed vibrates through an aperture when plucked, the mouth of the player acting as a soundbox; a few harmonic notes may be obtained by altering the shape of the mouth, as if saying the vowels. The Jews' harp is known in various forms in many parts of the world; among primitive peoples it is played to induce meditation, but it can be played loud enough to provide a strong rhythm for dancing, as in Sicily until only recently, and in Scotland as late as the eighteenth century.

Various reasons have been advanced for its Western name since it has no connection with the Jewish people, but like so much else about it, this

The Jews' Harp

so far remains a mystery. It appears among the sculptures of the fourteenth century Musicians' Gallery at Exeter Cathedral, and also among other instruments on the Crozier of William of Wykeham, appointed Bishop of Winchester in 1366. In Sicily a number of superstitions surround it, one being that a pregnant woman must not be allowed to hear it. Unfortunately, so much of the lore of the Old Faith here has been lost that we do not know what role it played here apart from its being played for ritual dancing. At a witchcraft trial in Scotland in 1590 one of the witches —a witch was no more than a member of a coven and professed follower of the Old Faith—described how a gathering of covens danced "endlong the churchyard" while one of them played on the trump (the old word for the Jews' harp).

The same player, Gelie Duncan, "upon the like trump did play the like dance before the King's Majesty". The musician was an important member of the coven, and was often the chief, or even the incarnate god himself, thus giving his instrument an odour of sanctity; sometimes this did not overcome the musicality of the worshippers, as one was accused thus: "Because the Devil played not so melodiously and well as thou crewit, thou took the instrument out of his mouth, then took him on the chaps therewith and played thyself thereon to the whole company." We do not know whether this was the Jews' harp, flute or pipes.

94

8   PERCUSSION

D R U M S H A V E N O T been played in church or chapel here except on special
occasions as part of an orchestra or military band. The bass and side drum,
with their summoning boom and urgent rattle, have for so long been part
of military music that it is no surprise that the Salvation Army have put
them to their own battles. The founder, General Booth, said he considered
the drum as sacred as cornet, organ or tambourine, and likened it to the
church bell, except that while the latter said "Come" the drum said "Fetch
'em!" Drum parts in Salvation Army music are composed with special
care, and in outdoor meetings the drum is the Mercy Seat to which
penitent sinners are called; after it was first so used, there were many
converts, and Fred Fry said: "We felt as if God had set his seal on the
drum." Before that there had been prejudice against an instrument so
much of the world. The first drummer was convicted for his "offence" in
Salisbury in 1879, but later became Mayor of that city.

The tambourine was also on active service; in 1881 General Booth had
likened the Salvation Army women to prophetesses leading the people
with music in processions of mercy; his article was illustrated with Miriam
playing a timbrel. After this, a commanding officer bought a tambourine
for his wife to play in procession "which filled the devil with disgust, the
newspaper with comments, the barracks with people, and helped sinners
into the fountain". Before a year was out, Army lasses had taken it up in
earnest, and one said: "I thought the tambourine a most natural means of
expressing our happiness, and I enjoyed banging my tambourine to the
glory of God." There are various techniques in tambourine playing to
make full use of the beat and the jingles, both separately and together. It
is interesting to recall how early Christians thought of it as a symbol of
moral rectitude, which is certainly appropriate to the Salvation Army.

Side and Bass Drums

Cymbals are also played in Salvation Army bands, again instruments to which the early Christians ascribed spiritual values, and which later Christians such as Sir William Leighton in 1613 thought suitable for praise:

> Praise Him with Simballs, loud Simballes
> With instruments were us'd by Jewes:

They were played by the Children of Israel, and were and still are in the rites of other faiths; in Tibet, for instance, the soft sounding broad rimmed cymbals played vertically are connected with worship of heavenly gods, and the smaller cymbals clashed one down on to the other with the gods of earth. There is no evidence of their being played in Christian worship in the past, but they are often depicted in the hands of angels in medieval and Renaissance pictures.

Drums did not appear in Europe until about the twelfth century, the first being the little tabor played together with a horn or whistle pipe, and now associated with Morris dancing, although they used to be played for all sorts of dancing and entertainment as well. The nakers followed, two small drums playing different tones, and the timbrel, all associated with

Tambourines

revelry. Other drums were military instruments, and one of these has become part of Ulster folklore. This is the Lambeg drum, an immensely large deep drum, which had been brought to Ireland in 1690 by the Dutch guards of William of Orange—ironically nearly all Roman Catholics. These drums had come to Europe from Turkey, and their players had always been virtuosos of drumming, using some of the techniques in practice among the Lambeg drummers today. The drums are played on July 12, anniversary of the Battle of the Boyne, each player contesting against the others to see who can keep up the longest, and playing until blood runs down from wrists and knuckles; one player is reputed to play with four sticks at once, a second pair being fixed to his wrists to come up in front of his hands. The drums have names, and are cared for as tenderly as favourite racehorses.

The most fascinating folk instrument in Ireland is the bodhran, pronounced "bowheran", which, like other apparently simple folk instruments, is complicated in its playing and construction. It is a large single membrane frame drum with the tightly stretched skin, preferably that of a goat, nailed on to the frame which is made of wood seasoned by being hung up in the smoke of a peat fire, which makes it very hard; the wood is then boiled and bent into shape, the rim supporting the skin being circular, and the other slightly oval: this means that the tension of the skin varies in different parts of its surface, and a skilled player can play a tune. In the past, players used the "naked" hand to play, using the fingers in various ways, while the fingers of the hand holding the cross piece at the back could alter the tone by pressing on the skin. This can still be done, but most players now use a "pin", a short two-headed stick held with the wrist bent towards the instrument; a skilled player scarcely moves his arm, wrist movement alone enabling him to hit all parts of the skin.

The old ones were sometimes very large; tradition has it that the arm holding the cross piece should be fully outstretched while the rim rests against the player's shoulder. Modern bodhrans are often made from the frames of sieves. The bodhran is said to have been found mostly along the west coast of Ireland; northern players called it "the bull". It is played for all sorts of folk music, and also for some folk customs, such as that of the New Year, when children go "collecting for the Wren"; the wren was a sacred bird to the druids, so the custom is very old.

The only other large frame drums of the Western world are those of

The Lambeg drum

The Bodhran

the Lapps and Greenlanders, which are believed to have magic powers. Legends abound about the bodhran itself, one being that at a certain time Catholics and Protestants quarrelled over a large drum which was divided between them, giving each side a bodhran.

The purpose of the noise-makers was to ward off evil spirits; these lurked at boundaries, seeking a chance to get in at the point where one thing ended and another began. The boundaries that needed guarding were not only physical ones such as thresholds, cross-roads, walls or rivers —there is a lot of old magic connected with bridge-building—but those of time and state, such as the longest and shortest day, or a birth, a wedding, and especially a death. On some of these occasions, noise-makers were to the fore and any instrument or thing that could be used as such were brought out: clappers, spoons, tongs and bellows, wooden saltboxes, tools of the trade. An instance is the annual Guild holiday of the Sweeps of London, which took place on May Day and joined up with the traditional Spring festivities. They all dressed up, some as women, and marched

Rough music

to Hampstead Heath accompanied by a Jack o' the Green on a donkey; Jack was a man covered in a framework of leafy branches, an old fertility symbol. The sweeps made a noise with anything they could, especially with their brushes beating against their shovels. In the same way, the Butchers' Guild beat marrowbones and cleavers at their festivities.

A more sinister music was the Rough Music or Charivari played at a demonstration to punish adultery in which effigies of the guilty pair or people dressed to look like them were tied on a donkey and the accompanying demonstrators made as much noise as they could. This was described by Nicholaus of Damascus in the last century B.C., and most recently in a news item in the *Daily Telegraph* in 1958. Known in Dorset as a Skimmity Ride, it had been witnessed by Thomas Hardy who describes it and its fatal consequences in *The Mayor of Casterbridge*, with

the "din of cleavers, tongs, kits, crouds, humstrums, serpents, rams' horns and other historical kinds of music . . ." (A kit was a small pocket fiddle, a croud probably a fiddle in this case, and a humstrum a four-stringed instrument rather like a rebec with a tin can for soundbox.)

Weddings were traditionally celebrated by a noisy assembly; in Ulster this was called a "dinning" and was an honour, since it was intended to drive away evil influences from the bridal pair; anything was used: horns, barrels, drums, and crackers as well as fiddles and pipes. In Hardy's *Far from the Madding Crowd* the newlywed Bathsheba and Gabriel Oak were similarly honoured on their return home; they met a group who cheered and let off a cannon, and at the same time there was "a hideous clang of music from a drum, tambourine, clarionet, serpent, hautboy, tenor viol and double bass—venerable wormeaten instruments which had celebrated in their own persons the victories of Marlborough under the fingers of the forefathers of those who played them now". The writer of the "Christen State of Matrimony" 1543, deplores such wedding customs: "They come with a great Noise of Harpes, Lutes, Kyttes, Basens and Drommes, wherewyth they Trouble the whole Church. . . ."

The Witches' Sabbaths of the Old Faith were often very noisy. In Lorraine in 1589 the women played whistle pipes, and a man a horse's skull "which he plays as a zither; another has a cudgel with which he strikes an oak tree . . . the Devil sings in a hoarse shout exactly as if he trumpeted through his nose . . . the whole troop shout, roar, bellow, howl, as if they were demented . . ." But others in France danced to the sound of tambourine and flute, and "they hear here every kind of instrument with such harmony that there is not a concert in the world that can equal it".

The Wedding Party

Trumpeter Sheard's cornet

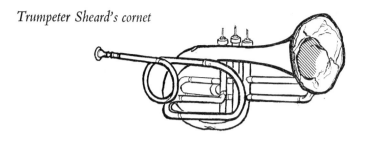

9

> The man must shut his eyes and blow his cornet, and believe while he plays
> that he is blowing salvation into somebody.
> *From the general rule for Salvation Army bands laid down in 1884 by General*
> *William Booth, founder of the Salvation Army.*

HERE, IN THE Salvation Army, instruments of music are seen as instruments for the salvation of the human soul, and amongst the many used by the Army the chief are the brass instruments. There are about 20,000 Salvation Army bandsmen in this country, and many more overseas, many of them of high musical standing; in addition, the Army publishes its own music, often composed by Salvationists, and makes its own instruments.

Present-day bands have, on the whole, the usual brass band instrumentation (contesting being so much a part of the brass band movement, it was necessary to have a uniform instrumentation to make judging fair). The instruments are members of the posthorn and bugle family, plus trombones, which are trumpets, and, especially important for the Salvation Army, drums.

Horns are usually made of metal and have an expanding bore—the inner profile—and a deep cupped mouthpiece; this gives them their mellow carrying sound. Brass band horns have a fairly narrow bore, flaring into a wide bell, except for the flügel horn, developed from the old bugle horn, which has a wider bore gradually expanding to the bell and a deeper conical mouthpiece and a more mellow tone.

Trumpets have a less conical bore, except for the bell, a shallower mouthpiece, and their tone is more brilliant; the trombone has a deeper mouthpiece and its strident tone strengthens the bass part of the brass band. All brass instruments are lip reed, that is, the sound is caused by the vibration of the player's lips across the mouthpiece; by altering the tension of his lips, he can sound harmonics of the fundamental or key note of the instrument, the number depending on the length of the tube (see page 121). There have been various experiments to increase the range of notes and fill out the scale: one of these, the trombone, was strikingly successful, being, roughly speaking, a folded trumpet with a sliding section on one of the folds, that could lengthen the whole tube at will. There are seven positions of the slide, each giving a different fundamental and set of harmonics, enabling the trombone to play a chromatic scale. The first trombones were made in the fourteenth century, for church music in the first place, and have not changed in essentials.

It was not until the early nineteenth century that any other revolutionary development took place in brass instruments. Then the application of keyed holes was quickly followed by the invention of the valve which, on depressing a piston or key, let in an extra length of valve-tubing to the whole. Bandsmen and makers all over Europe experimented with valves, with the result that bands in different countries favour different mechanisms and groupings of instruments. In this country, the brass band movement adopted the Saxhorns, a family of horns patented in Paris by Adolph Sax in 1846. Of these, the leading melody instruments are the cornets; there are eight or nine B flat cornets, four solo, one "repiano" (from *ripieno* meaning supplementary), two second, and one or two third, as well as the E flat soprano cornet for very high parts. The flügel horn enriches the melody instruments.

There are three E flat tenor horns, known to bandsmen as "horns", playing solo and first and second parts. Next come two baritones and two euphoniums, both in B flat; the baritone has a smaller bore and lighter tone, and is better for fast passages, and the euphonium a fuller tone; they are the chief melody instruments of the bass section. These are supported by the basses or tubas, two in E flat, and often the big BB flat contrabass, or double B, as it is known. These are transposing instruments, that is, the music for each part is scored in the treble clef but played lower by ninths or sixths. The two tenor B flat trombones play at the same pitch as the euphonium, and the bass trombone is in G or F and the only instrument to have music scored in the bass clef.

The Salvation Army has a number of famous bands, many of which have campaigned all over the world. Chalk Farm is the most travelled corps band, being the first to go abroad. The Salvation Army Household Troops Band, then called the Band of the Life Guards, was formed in 1885 to accompany a band of cadets going into action on what was known as the Great Kent March; as a result of this, a permanent band was set up for this sort of campaigning. Wearing all sorts of uniforms, and enduring much hardship—in twelve months they covered 3,000 miles, half of it on foot, travelling lower deck, and some being imprisoned on the way—they went to America, Canada and Europe before 1891. Then they were disbanded, and the International Staff Band was formed from a junior band of office boys and junior clerks at the Army's International Centre in London. At that time there was opposition to the Army, and these boys were roughly handled by the police when an Army demonstration was broken up; however, this made them stand all the firmer, and their band was later led by outstanding musician Salvationists.

Apart from the headquarters bands and the leading corps bands, there are hundreds of other small bands up and down the country—indeed, all over the world—making do with what instruments they have, and always trying to do better. The discipline is strict, both as to personal conduct and as to the demands made on the bandsmen and women by practice time and by campaigning.

Now that the Salvation Army is well known and respected, the worst it meets on the streets is apathy, but in the early days Salvationists met with active opposition from the roughest sections of the crowd, and from respectable citizens and the law on a charge of "rabble rousing". The first brass players came out to overcome this opposition: in 1878 a group of Salvationists, or "disorderly characters" as some said, were holding outdoor evangelistic meetings in Salisbury, with a great deal of noisy, violent

Tenor trombone   *Cornet*

opposition; one night a respected citizen and local preacher, Charles Fry, and his three sons came to the meeting bringing with them two cornets, a trombone and a euphonium. The music of these, like that of other players elsewhere, was so successful in commanding the attention of the crowd and quietening their wildness that General Booth asked the family to play at other meetings, Charles Fry giving up his business to do so. Other players joined them, and at one time the Hallelujah Minstrels, as they were then called, had three cornets, baritone, trombone, euphonium and bass drum. One of the cornettists was Arthur Sheard, later to be called Trumpeter Sheard and to accompany General Booth on many campaigns. During one of these he was taken to court for playing in the market-place in Derby; forty years later he came back, this time to visit a local corps with a band of forty strong, and once more he played in the market-place, the same tune and on the same cornet (see p.103), and the local paper reported that Trumpeter Sheard "had got his own back". He retired from

Tenor horn, usually known as the horn

Double Bass, or contrabass tuba

campaigning in 1940 at eighty-two. The drummer of the Hallelujah Minstrels was prosecuted in Salisbury and later became mayor of the same city.

Charles Fry died after two years of campaigning and the band broke up; but by then the value of music was fully realized. All sorts of bands flourished: drum and fife, brass, string, and some mixtures such as Mexborough's violin, flute, bell and huntsman's horn. The brass bands were the most suitable, and by 1883 there were 400 in the British Isles. The first corps to have its own band was Consett in County Durham, the four pioneer members going into action at Christmas 1879. The first woman cornettist in band history took her place in Portsmouth Band, joined later by Captain Case and his daughters and their mother with the cymbals.

At first, the bands were used to help the singing, and they played all sorts of music, popular tunes, music supplied by outside publishers, and old hymn tunes, and all at different pitches and harmonies. Then Fred, Charles Fry's son, was given the task of producing music suitable for the increasing number of bands; this he did, composing and printing it himself on an old printing press and with some old music type given up as useless. Two years later the Army set up its own music department, outside music being forbidden; this resulted, as in the brass band movement as a whole, in composers rising from the ranks.

Salvation Army music was reviewed in 1916. Its purposes were determined as three-fold; to attract, to accompany congregational singing, and to speak directly to the hearts of the people. Instrumental music has over the centuries been composed and played to the glory of God, but here, in this third purpose, the instruments play a special role, especially the brass which, making music by the player's own lips and breath, establishes the closest link of any save the flute between player and instrument. Catherine Booth, the Army Mother, echoed Luther's words when she said that she had always regarded music as belonging to God, and continued:

> ". . . and while the bandsmen of the Salvation Army realize it to be as much their service to blow an instrument as it is to sing, pray or speak, and while they do so in the same spirit, I am persuaded it will become an ever increasing power amongst us."

However, the Salvation Army were not the first to use brass instruments in religious service. The church bands welcomed any instrumentalist whatever the previous association of his instrument. Among these were the key bugle and ophicleide; the key bugle had been invented by an army bandmaster in 1810, and was an army bugle with finger holes controlled by keys, at first five and later six; in this way, the tube was shortened by opening holes, each successive shorter length having its higher key note and limited range of harmonics; a two-octave chromatic scale could be played. Key bugles, apart from their army use, came into early brass bands, and were also played as coaching horns. The ophicleide was the bass keyed bugle, and took the place of the serpent, especially in France where it was often the only instrument playing with the choir during Mass.

The serpent was another bass instrument of the early church bands. It was a large serpentine horn made of wood with a cupped mouthpiece on a metal crook, first made in France in the sixteenth century for playing in church; there it played during the liturgy. Guy de Maupassant describes a village service of the last century where "the Cantors and the Serpent

The keyed bugle

The Ophicleide

struck up with one accord" and after an emotional service, "the very Serpent seemed to croak as if it, too, had been weeping".

It was a member of eighteenth-century military bands here, as well as church bands. The finger holes were of necessity wide apart, and the instrument was difficult to play, so its bass part was often taken over by the bass viol; nevertheless, it had its own charm: "There's things worse than serpents," says one of Hardy's musicians. "Old things pass away, 'tis true; but a serpent was a good old note: a deep rich note was the serpent."

Trombone and cornet (in its early form as the cornopean) also played in church bands, although they, like the bugle, were a later innovation. In Puddletown in Dorset a rival band was set up to the old band which had the traditional clarinet, flute, bassoon and strings; the Scorpion Band, as it was called, had clarinet, cornopean and bass drum, but it is unlikely they were asked to play in church. In Birdham, Sussex, there was a transitional band of cornet, violin and harmonium.

The trombone was re-introduced into military music by German musicians in the eighteenth century. Previously to this, it had fallen into disuse here; an inventory of the contents of Canterbury Cathedral church reports: "In one of these chests are contained only two brass sackbuts not

The Serpent

us'd for a grete number of years past . . ." Sackbut is the old name, from the Spanish *sacar bucha*—"to draw" and "a tube"; it had a smaller bore than the modern trombone and it could be played with a soft tone which teamed well with the delicate note of the cornett and the voices which both were used to accompany in church. They also played for processional music, and were found in the service of kings and nobles, where they were played at a time when other instruments were making them old-fashioned. By the end of the seventeenth century the new French hautboy, the curtal and the bass hautboy were taking their place in processional music. There were "shagbuts and cornitors" at the funeral of James I, and the music of Elizabeth's Chapel Royal was augmented for festivals by other instruments such as "cornits, sackbuts, ect". Both Henry VIII and his father maintained sackbut players, and earlier still, at the Council of Constance, a meeting of "all Christendom" in 1414–18, not only did the English choristers charm their hearers, but the crowd were impressed by the four English sacbutters who played through the town at the time of vespers.

The cornett went out of fashion earlier than the sacbut; John Evelyn, writing in his diary in 1662 laments that in the music of the Chapel Royal "no more is heard the cornett which gave life to the organ. That instrument quite left off on which the English were so skilful". Evidently it was played with the organ for some religious services, supplying a tone which the organ then lacked. The cornett, which can now be heard again played by musicians specializing in Renaissance and medieval music, is a gently curving, six sided horn, made of ivory, or wood bound with leather, and with a small, shallow cupped mouthpiece. It has six holes and a thumb hole at the back; the largest cornett, the tenor—they were played in a "nest" of three—has a seventh hole with a swallow-tail key. The mute cornett is straight, with the mouthpiece inside the tube, and has a muted note. The cornett was well suited to accompany church singing, since all contemporary writers agree that it sounded more like the human voice than any other instrument; to Mersenne it suggested a ray of sunshine, and Praetorius considered it gentle and sweet.

Cornett players were attached to most cathedrals in the fifteenth and sixteenth centuries; there were two on the list of officers for Canterbury Cathedral in 1532. The cornett is thought to have developed from the watchmen's horns, and has a cousin in the Scandinavian folk instruments, bukkehorns, goats' and cows' horns with fingerholes. Such horns appear in early MSS., played in the presence of King David.

The trumpet, in many religions possessing so potent a magic, became in the West the instrument played in the service of kings and princes. During the Middle Ages it was also played in church processions on holy

Sackbuts and cornetts, 16th-century

A 13th-century bishop and his trumpets

days, and during the Mass at the Showing of the Host, the focal point of the service when the priest shows the congregation the consecrated bread and wine. This solemn moment was made more awesome by the loud braying note of the medieval trumpet. It was also played sometimes at the Mysteries, by trumpeters accompanying the armies of Christ, and for the Last Trump at the Day of Judgement.

The animal horns, and their metal counterparts were used by country people to call their herds and for hunting. If we accept Robin Goodfellow as being a later Horned God or Pan, then he also carries and presumably calls up his worshippers with a horn; he wears one on the cover of a seventeenth-century book about his *Mad Prankes and Merry Iests*. By then he is a joke, a sort of fairy creature, but his origin as a god is clear from the picture; he dances in a ring of eleven worshippers; a twelfth plays the music, apparently some sort of shawm; this makes thirteen in all, the number of people in a coven or church, counting the god himself.

The fairies themselves, whose horns are heard sounding in old ballads, were, according to some scholars, not pretty fancies but descendants of

the Bronze Age people who took refuge from the Iron Age Celtic in-
vaders in the most wild and inaccessible parts of Western Europe and
Great Britain, such as the Highlands—there is a wealth of Scots faerie
ballads and stories—parts of the Pennines, and Dartmoor. Here they lived
in fairy houses, Stone Age beehive dwellings of which a few survive, and
were credited with magic powers by the newcomers. They continued to
follow the Old Faith until they were finally absorbed into whichever
country they lived in. There are many accounts and pictures of meetings
with fairies, with talk of changelings and fairy godmothers, all of which
makes sense.

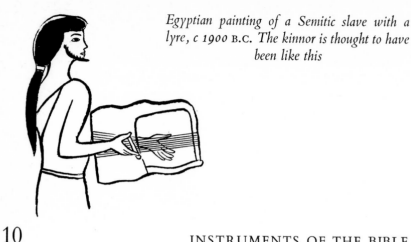

Egyptian painting of a Semitic slave with a lyre, c 1900 B.C. The kinnor is thought to have been like this

10 INSTRUMENTS OF THE BIBLE

Praise him with the sound of the trumpet:
Praise him with the psaltery and harp.
Praise him with the timbrel and dance:
Praise him with the stringed instruments and organs.
Praise him upon the loud cymbals:
Praise him upon the high-sounding cymbals.

Psalm 150.

THIS PSALM and other passages from the Old Testament have led people to imagine the Children of Israel playing the instruments of medieval Europe. In fact, the translators of the Authorized and Revised versions neither knew nor could have known all the instruments the Jews actually played; the Holy Scriptures from which the translations were made were not illustrated, the scribes being forbidden for religious reasons to depict anything living or made by man. Nor could the translators have studied the paintings and sculptures of neighbouring civilizations such as Egypt and Mesopotamia, since most of these things were as yet unknown to the West. Therefore they did the best they could, and translated such instruments as they did not know as those which to them were old-fashioned, like the psaltery, or connected with worship, like the organ. However,

Egyptian long flute, before 2000 B.C.
The Ugab, like many other Middle
Eastern flutes, was probably like this
(compare also p. 80)

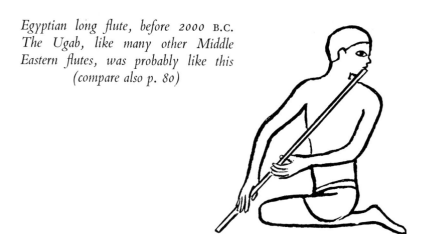

since then scholars have not only translated the Scriptures with greater accuracy, but have studied the civilizations of the Jews and their neighbours in the light of new discoveries, and can come a little nearer to the truth about the instruments.

From about 2,000 to 1,000 B.C., the Jews were a nomadic people, and sang and played the appropriate instruments for praise, mourning, battle, and so on. The first to be mentioned (Genesis 4:21) is the kinnor, translated as harp, which was probably a small lyre with strings made of sheep's gut. David's harp was probably a kinnor, and so were those which the exiled Jews hung on willow trees because they could only be played for joyful occasions. The ugab, mentioned at the same time, and translated as organ, was probably a long, deep-sounding vertical flute. The tof was a wide frame drum, still found in the East, and nearly always played by women: it was the "timbrel" played by Miriam and Jephthah's daughter. The pa'amon was the small bell or jingle on the priest's robe to ward off evil (see page 46). The hasosra were the silver trumpets, always played in pairs as in the ritual of many other faiths, and ordered to be played to call God to his people (Numbers 10:1–2; 9–10). The shofar was and is the sacred horn, made from the horn of a goat or ram, steamed until soft and then straightened at the narrow end. It was played by the priests at the time of the New Moon, and for Fast Days and the New Year. The walls of

Jericho were brought down—excavations show that they really did tumble down—by the sound of the shofarot.

During the reigns of David and Solomon, Israel was established as a kingdom, set at the junction of important trade routes and open to travellers from all over the known world; Solomon took to wife princesses from many kingdoms, who brought among their entourages musicians and their instruments. The music of the Temple was provided by selected Levites—members of the priestly caste—who were especially trained at an academy of religious music, and other instruments were added.

Egyptian round and quadrilateral tambourines, probably similar to the Tof

The nevel was probably a harp, larger than the kinnor, and with a deeper and louder tone, since it had heavier gut strings; it was held with the rounded body, or sound-box, above the strings, and resembled in outline the skin bottle also called nevel. The asor was a ten-stringed instrument, probably a zither of Phoenician origin, with plucked strings stretched over a square sound-box; this is translated as psaltery, and so called by the early Christians; St. Jerome, in a letter to one of his brethren in about A.D. 400, drew it, and wrote: "It has ten strings as it is written: I shall praise you on the ten-stringed Psaltery."

Selslim and msiltayim were the cymbals; the former were probably of two kinds, one wide-rimmed with small bosses and played vertically with a skimming movement, and a soft sound, and the other narrow-rimmed with large bosses and struck horizontally with a clash. The msiltayim were probably small cymbals fixed to clappers made from the two prongs of a split cane. Halil and abub, translated as flutes, were more likely reed pipes. Traditionally there was in the Temple a reed pipe from the time of Moses, and neighbouring countries all had reed pipes, usually played in pairs, and with double reeds like the oboe. After the establishment of the Second Temple about 500 years B.C., pipes were played at twelve rituals during the year; at first they were cylindrical,

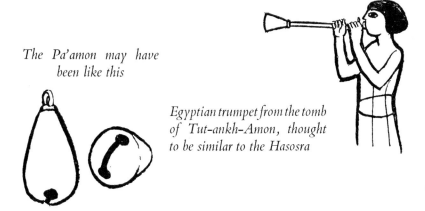

The Pa'amon may have been like this

Egyptian trumpet from the tomb of Tut-ankh-Amon, thought to be similar to the Hasosra

but later became conical and similar to the Arabian shawm. It is just possible that there was a Greek hydraulus, or water organ, in the Third Temple just before its destruction, but this was never a Jewish instrument. Other Old Hebrew words, once thought to designate instruments, are now thought to be musical terms or directions.

After the destruction of the Third Temple and the scattering of the people, they vowed that there would be no more priests—the rabbi is a teacher, not a priest—and no more instruments played until the Temple be built once more. As we have seen, this broke down in Europe at times, and the Liberal or Reformed Synagogue admits the organ. The only ancient ritual instrument that survived the cruel centuries of dispersal and persecution

117

*Egyptian harp with skin covered sound box;
it is thought the Nevel was like this*

*Phoenician instrument with ten strings,
possibly like the ten-stringed psaltery of the
Old Testament (from a vase)*

Egyptian double pipes with single reeds

was the shofar, which continues to be sounded at the New Moon services of the Orthodox Synagogue; and in all synagogues, as Sachs says: "New Year's and the Day of Atonement end with the violent, awe-inspiring blasts of the traditional shofar." The shofar can sound the second and third harmonics and there are four traditional blasts or fanfares, the final being the Tqia Gdola or "great blast" when the player can "flip up" to the fourth harmonic.

Like other ritual horns of great antiquity, its old magic clings: at one time it could not be seen by the worshippers, but was sounded "off-stage"; women and children, unlike the men, are not obliged to listen—in the long past they were not allowed to, as in some primitive places today. It is the only instrument played in the Western world that has this long unbroken and intimate connection with the rituals and faith of its people: it has become further sanctified by the endurance of the ancient faith and the people who brought to the Western countries, where they have so often been fugitives, so much that has enriched our now common culture and spiritual life.

The Shofar

Book List

GENERAL REFERENCE

GROVE, *Dictionary of Music and Musicians*. Macmillan.

Oxford History of Music. Oxford University Press.

SCHOLES, *Oxford Companion to Music*. Oxford University Press.

BAINES, ANTHONY (ed.), *The Pelican Book of Musical Instruments*. Penguin Books.

OTHER BOOKS

BAINES, ANTHONY, *Woodwind Instruments and their History*. Faber & Faber.

BENADE, ARTHUR, *Horns, Strings and Harmony* (for the physics of sound). Doubleday.

BOON, BRINDLEY, *Play the Music, Play* (the story of the Salvation Army music). Salvation Publishing & Supplies, London, W.C.1.

CARSE, ADAM. *Musical Wind Instruments*. Da Capo Press.

CLUTTON, CECIL, and NILAND, AUSTIN, *The British Organ*. Batsford.

GALPIN, F. W., *Old English Instruments of Music*. Methuen.

HARRISON, FRANK, and RIMMER, JOAN, *European Musical Instruments*. Studio Vista.

MACDERMOTT, K. H., *Sussex Church Music of the Past*; *The Old Church Gallery Minstrels*.

MORELL, R. CONYERS, *The Romance of our Old Village Choirs*.

MORRISS, ERNEST, *Tintinnabula*; *History and Art of Change Ringing*; *Legends o' the Bells*.

MURRAY, MARGARET A., *The God of the Witches*. Sampson Low.

PHILLIPS, C. E., *The Singing Church*. Faber.

ROUTLEY, ERIK, *The Church and Music*. Duckworth.

SACHS, KURT, *The History of Musical Instruments*. Dent.

SUMNER, WILLIAM L., *The Organ*. Macdonald.

WILLIAMS, C. F. ABDY, *The Study of the Organ*. Walter Scott Publishing Co.

Appendix

The Diatonic scale is the division of the octave into eight notes, making the major and minor scales upon which most Western music is based.

Diatonic scale of G Major.

The Chromatic scale divides the octave into thirteen semitones.

Chromatic scale of G.

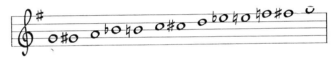

The Harmonic scale is made up of harmonics, or overtones, of the Tonic or key-note. The harmonics of any note are heard simultaneously, but certain instruments give greater or lesser value to some of them. Other instruments, e.g. the bugle, can produce the harmonics separately; bugle calls are made up of these notes.

Harmonic scale of G.

H

Organisations useful to the student

The British Institute of Recorded Sound: national collection of sound recordings. 29 Exhibition Road, S.W.7.

The English Folk Dance and Song Society: information on folk dance and song, folklore, etc.; recordings; library. Cecil Sharp House, 2 Regent's Park Road, N.W.1.

The Galpin Society: information on the history of musical instruments; lectures; recitals; demonstrations. Hon. Sec. Jeremy Montagu, 7 Pickwick Road, S.E.21.

Museums and Collections

BRIGHTON MUNICIPAL MUSEUM (*the Spencer Collection*)

CASTLE MUSEUM, York.

FOLK MUSEUM, Cambridge.

GLEN, BAGPIPE MAKER, Edinburgh.

HORNIMAN MUSEUM, Forest Hill, S.E.23.

LUTON BOROUGH MUSEUM (*the Ridley Collection of wind instruments*).

PAYTON'S MUSIC STORES, Islington High Street, N.1.

PITT RIVERS MUSEUM, Oxford (*2–4 p.m. only*).

REID SCHOOL OF MUSIC, Edinburgh.

ROYAL COLLEGE OF MUSIC, Kensington, S.W.7 (*term-time only*).

ROYAL SCOTTISH MUSEUM, Edinburgh.

RUSHWORTH AND DREAPER, music dealers, Liverpool.

SALVATION ARMY MUSEUM, Congress Hall, Linscott Road, Clapton, E.5.

THE WELSH FOLK MUSEUM, St. Fagan's Castle, Cardiff.

VICTORIA AND ALBERT MUSEUM, Kensington, S.W.7.

List of the Stops
on Coventry Cathedral Organ, 1962

The new organ in Coventry Cathedral was made by Harrison & Harrison, 1962.

GREAT (15 stops)

Double Diapason
Bourdon
Open Diapason I
Open Diapason II
Spitzflute
Stopped Diapason
Octave
Gemshorn
Octave Quint
Super Octave
Mixture IV
Cornet II–V
Double Trumpet
Trumpet
Clarion

Choir/Great
Swell/Great
Solo/Great

CHOIR (13 stops)

Claribel Flute
Diapason
Harmonic Flute
Gedacht
Dulciana
Principal
Rohr Flute
Nazard
Fifteenth
Block Flute
Tierce
Mixture V
Cromorne

Tremulant
Swell/Choir
Solo/Choir

PEDAL (20 stops)

Sub Bourdon
Open Wood
Open Metal
Diapason
Sub Bass
Dulciana
Principal
Spitzflute
Twelfth
Fifteenth
Rohr Flute
Open Flute
Mixture IV

Bombardon
Ophicleide
Fagotto
Posaune
Bassoon
Schalmei
Kornett

Choir/Pedal
Great/Pedal
Swell/Pedal
Solo/Pedal
Great/Pedal combinations coupled

123

SWELL (13 stops)
 enclosed
Quintadena
Hohl Flute
Viola
Celeste AA $\sharp$
Principal
Spitzflute
Fifteenth
Sesquialtera II
Mixture IV
Oboe
Contra Fagotto
Trumpet
Clarion

Tremulant
Octave
Solo/Swell

SOLO (12 stops)
 enclosed except for Orchestral trumpets
Diapason
Rohr Flute
Viole
Viole Celeste
Octave
Open Flute
Wald Flute
Sifflöte
Mixture IV
Corno di Bassetto
Orchestral Trumpet
Orchestral Clarion

Tremulant

Couplers and other devices.

A total of 73 speaking stops, and 15 couplers, etc.

Both Solo and Swell are enclosed, and situated on the south side of the Cathedral. Great is on the north side, and Pedal and Choir have pipes distributed between north and south, some of which are visible.

List of the Stops
on St. Paul's Organ, 1697

A list of the stops of Father Smith's organ for St. Paul's Cathedral 1697 (from his own specifications).

GREAT
Open Diapason
Open Diapason
Stop Diapason
Principall
Hol Fleut
Great Twelfth
ffifteenth
Small Twelfth
Cornet
Mixture
Sesquialtera
Trumpet

CHAYRE (choir)
Quinta Dena Diapason
Stop Diapason
Principall
Hol Fleut
Great Twelfth
Fifteenth
Cimball
Voice Humaine
Crum Horne

ECCHO
Diapason
Principall
Nason
ffifteenth
Cornet
Trumpet

The two original cases contain only a few of the pipes now in use; other pipes can be seen from various points of the Whispering Gallery.

A RINGERS' RHYME

Those that do heare intend to ringe
Let them consider first this thing:
If that they do a bell turn ore
Fourepence to pay therefore:
If any ring with hat or spur
Twopence to pay by this order:
If any chance to curse or swear
Fourepence to pay and eke forbere.

By John Burnell, 1663, Culmington Church,
Shropshire.

A medieval Latin rhyme about the bell.

En ego campana, nunquam denuncio vana,
Behold! I, the bell, never proclaim vain things,

Laudo Deum verum, plebem voco, congrego clarum,
I praise the true God, I summon the people, I gather the clergy,

Defunctus plango, viros voco, fulmina frango,
I toll for the dead, I call the living, I shatter the thunderbolts,

Vox mea, vox vitae, voco vos ad sacra venite,
My voice, voice of life, I call you, come to divine worship,

Sanctos collando, tonitrua fugo, funera claudo,
I praise the holy, I put the thunder to flight, I conclude funeral rites,

Funera plango, fulgura frango, Sabbatha pango,
I toll for funerals, I shatter the lightning, I mark the Sabbath,

Excito lentos, dissipo ventos, paco cruentos.
I arouse the lazy, I disperse the winds, I pacify the bloodthirsty.

Read aloud in Latin, this poem has the ring and swing of the bells.

Index

		Text	Illustration
A	Abub.	117	118
	Alexandre	33	
	American organ	32, 92, 93	
	André	91	
	Angel Adjutant the	91	90
	Anthem	23, 24	
	Apollo	9, 16, 88	
	Asor	116	118
B	Bach	53	
	Bach organ	see organ	
	bagpipes	34, 71, 82, 83	83
	bands, brass	32, 68, 103–105	
	Church	27–28, 68–69, 78–80, 85–86, 108–109	26, 78
	Salvation Army	32, 96, 103, 105–108	30–31
	Baptists	93	
	Bardic instruments	74, 75, 76	34, 74, 75, 76
	bards	75, 76, 77	
	baritone	104	31
	barrel organ	see organ	
	bassoon	78, 79, 80	78, 79
	bass viol (viola da gamba)	69, 80, 85, 88	29
	bells:	10–11, 12, 14, 22, 23, 29, 35 et seq., 95, 115	see under individual bells
	animals'	44, 45	44
	baptism and blessing of	42, 43	
	Bourdon	35, 36	35
	buffeted	42	
	casting of	37, 39	
	Celtic	10, 14, 44	45
	church	10, 12, 14, 22, 23, 26, 29, 35, 77, 95	14, 36, 37
	curfew	41	
	foundries	36–37	
	hand	44, 107	44
	Houseling	42	
	jingle	7, 10, 34, 45, 115	7, 46, 11

		Text	*Illustration*
	Latin rhyme on	126	
	Passing	42	
	powers of	10, 40, 41, 42, 43, 44, 45, 46	
	ringers and ringing of	23, 26, 38, 39, 126	37
	Sanctus (sacristy)	16, 40	41
	storm	43	
	tuned	13, 16, 40	11, 13, 17
	Beltane	84	
	Bible regal	81	81
	Big Ben	36	35
	bodhran	97–99	99
	Booth, William	95, 103, 106	
	Catherine	108	
	bowed lyre	*see* lyre	
	bow, musical	8, 9	9
	brass	114 et seq.	*see under* individual instruments
	bucium	8	8
	bugle:	103, 104	
	key	108	109
	bukkehorn	111	
	Byrd, William	23	
C	Cadi	42	
	campanology	26, 32	
	carillon	29, 40	
	Cavaillé-Coll	64	
	'cello	27, 69, 70	26
	chapel	12, 28, 62, 88, 89, 93	
	Chapel Royal	20, 23, 24, 25, 70, 110	
	change ringing	23, 38–39	
	Charivari	100	100–101
	Charles I	25	
	Charles II	24, 70	
	chair (choir) organ	*see* organ	
	Childermass	42	
	Church, Anglican	13, 23, 27, 31, 93	
	Catholic	13, 20, 26, 29, 40, 42, 56, 97, 99	
	Celtic	10, 44	
	Early	9, 10, 31, 77, 95, 96, 116	
	Lutheran	21	
	Reformed	21	
	clappers	42, 99	
	clarinet	27, 78–79, 101, 109	78, 79
	Clarsach	34, 76	76
	Commonwealth	57, 79	

		Text	Illustration
	concertina	90–91	90
	cornet	104, 106, 109	30, 103, 106
	cornett	16, 23, 70, 110–111	17, 111
	cornopean	109	
	coven	94, 112	19–20
	Cromwell, Oliver	57	
	Croyland Abbey bells	14, 39	
	crwth	34, 74–75, 101	75
	cymbals	9, 96, 114, 116, 117	
D	Dallam, Thomas	57, 63	
	Robert	57, 58	
	David, King	10, 15, 16, 75, 88, 111, 116	11, 17
	Debain	91	
	Denner, Johann	78	
	dinning	101	
	Dixon, Colonel	66	
	double bass ('Grandmother Fiddle')	69, 102	
	double bass (contra bass tuba)	104–105	107
	drums, bass	95, 109	31, 96
	biblical	115	116
	folk	7, 8, 9, 96, 101–102	7, 10, 102
	Lambeg	97	98
	sacred	9	
	Salvation Army	32, 95, 103, 107	31, 96
	side	95	96
	slit		10
	'drum log'	73	
	Duddyngton, Antony	56	
	Dyer, John	55	
E	Eccho	see organ	
	Edward VI	20, 21	
	Elgar, Edward	34	
	Elizabeth I	21, 23, 82	
	England family	61	
	euphonium	104, 106	31
	Evans	92	
F	Fairies	112–113	
	fiddle:	18, 27, 68–69, 71, 74, 101	26, 70
	Minnesinger	71	70
	flügelhorn	103–104	
	flute:	27, 50, 80, 85–86, 94, 102, 107, 109	26, 85
	long	115	8, 115

		Text	Illustration
	Fry, Charles	106, 107	
	Fred	95, 107	
G	gallery choirs	27, 31	26
	Gauntlett, Henry	62	
	Gibbons, Orlando	22, 23	
	Great organ	see organ	
	Great Paul	35, 36	
	Great Tom	36	
	guilds	16, 99, 100	
	guimbard (Jew's harp)	93	94
	guitar	17, 32	
H	Halberstadt organ bellows		54
	halil	117	
	Hallelujah minstrels	106–107	
	Hallowmass	42	
	Happy Eliza	32, 68	69
	harmonica:	32, 90	
	bellows	91	
	harmonium	32, 88, 91–92, 95, 109	33, 91, 92
	harps:	9, 10, 16	17
	Biblical	115–116	118
	English	74, 76–77, 86, 102	76
	ground	8	76
	Irish	34, 76	76
	Welsh	34, 75	34
	Harris, Renatus	58, 59, 61	
	organ by		60
	Harris, John	61	
	Harrison, Arthur	66	
	Harrison & Harrison	65, 123	
	hasosra	115	117
J	Jacob, Benjamin	61	
	Jewish faith	9, 30–31, 114 et seq.	
	instruments	114 et seq.	114, 117, 119
	Jew's harp	11, 20, 93–94	94
	(Jew's trump)		
	Jordans, Abraham	61	
	Joy Strings	32	
K	key bugle	108	109
	kit (kytte)	101, 102	
	kinnor	115, 116	114
L	lagerphone	8	
	Lambeg drum	97	98

		Text	*Illustration*
	Landini	55	
	Levites	70, 116	
	lira	16	17
	lute	70, 102	102
	Luther, Martin	20, 21, 108	
	lyre:	9, 74	10
	bowed	74–75	75
M	MacDermott, Rev.	93	
	Mace, Thomas	58	
	marine trumpet	*see* Tromba Marina	
	Mass	16, 20, 21, 23, 26, 56, 108, 112	
	Mersenne	111	
	metrical psalms	21, 24	
	Minnesinger fiddle	71	70
	mixture stops	50	
	monochord	14, 16, 72–73	17, 72
	Morris dances	7, 45, 87, 96	7
	msiltayim	116	
	musickers	12, 27, 31, 62, 68, 79, 85,	26, 78
	(musicianers)	88, 109	
	Mustel	91–92	
	mutation stops	50	
	Mysteries	14, 15, 112	
	(miracle plays)		
N	nakers	96	102
	nevel	116	118
	noise-makers	7, 99–102	
O	oboe	27, 78, 80	79, 80
	Old Faith (Old Religion)	11, 16, 20, 71, 83–84, 86–87, 94, 102, 113	
	ophicleide	108	109
	organ:	7, 12, 13, 14, 15, 19, 20, 22, 23, 24, 25, 28–29, 30, 31, 32–33, 47 et seq., 67, 71, 81, 114, 115	
	Bach	28, 33	
	barrel	63	63
	Carisbrooke	24	25
	chair (choir)	20, 25, 49, 53, 57, 58, 61, 62	
	Coventry Cathedral	66, 123	65
	Eccho	25–26, 28, 58, 61	
	great	20, 25, 49, 53, 56, 57, 58, 61, 62	
	Pedal	28, 49, 53, 61, 62	

	Text	Illustration
portative	55	55
positive	14, 16, 20, 23, 55, 56	13, 17, 53, 56
regal	58, 80–81	81
St. Paul's Cathedral	47–48, 58, 125	Frontispiece
Solo	49	
Swell	28, 49, 61, 62	
organ cases:	26, 28, 47, 57, 66, 67	see below
Coventry Cathedral	66, 123	65
Framlingham		59
Jesus College, Cambridge		66
St. James's, Piccadilly		60
St. Paul's Cathedral	45, 49	Frontispiece
organ pipes:	14, 19, 33, 47–49, 50, 52, 54, 56–57, 59, 60, 61, 63, 65, 66	48, 52
diapason	33, 50, 64	
flue	50, 53	52
reed	50, 52, 58	52
organ stops:	19, 49, 50, 56–57, 58, 61, 62 123–125	51
flute tone	50	
mixture	50	
mutation	50	
reed tone	50, 52, 58, 61	
string tone	50 52	
le Organer, Hugh	55	
organistrum	13, 14, 71–72	13, 72
orgues expressifs	32, 91	
pa'amon	115	117
Palestrina	15	
panpipes	16, 87–88	17, 88
pibcorn	82	82
piob mor	82–83	83
pipes, pipe and tabor	7, 20, 34, 87, 96	7, 87
organ	see organ	
reed	83–84	84
whistle	85, 87, 96	7, 87
pitch-pipe	27, 88–89	89
Plainsong (plain chant)	13, 31, 33	
polyphony	15, 21, 72	
portative	see organ	
positive	see organ	
Protestants	21, 22, 23, 99	

		Text	Illustration
	psalms	13, 21, 22, 26–27, 89	
	psaltery	10, 77, 116	77, reverse of frontispiece, 118
	Pugin, Henry	66	
	Purcell, Henry	28, 80	
	Puritans	12, 22, 24, 57	
Q	quire organ	*see* chair organ	
R	ram's horn	101, 115	
	rattle	8	
	rebec	34, 71, 74, 101	71, 102
	recorder	86	86
	reeds:	78 et seq., 117–118	*see under* individual instruments
	double	78, 83, 117	*see under* individual instruments
	free	33, 90 et seq.	
	ribbon	8, 9	84
	single	78, 83, 117	82, 84
	stops	*see* organ	
	Reformation	21, 22, 29, 62	
	Regal	58, 80–81	81
	Renaissance	23, 33, 51, 65	
	Restoration	24, 70	
	ringers and ringing	*see* bells	
	rotta (rote)	74	74
	Rough Music	100–101	100–101
S	sackbut	70, 109–110	111
	St. Augustine	13	
	St. Columba's bell	10	
	St. Dunstan	53	
	St. Egbert	40	
	St. Garmon's bell		45
	St. Jerome	77, 116	
	St. Moluag's bell		45
	St. Ninian	44	
	St. Patrick	44	
	St. Patrick's bell	14	45
	St. Paul's Cathedral	23, 35–36, 47, 49	
	St. Paul's organ	*see* organ	
	Salvation Army	32, 68, 90–91, 95–96, 103, 105–108	30–31
	Sax, Adolph	104	
	Saxhorns	104	
	scales	121	
	scrapers	8	

		Text	Illustration
	selslim	116	
	serpent	27, 101, 108–109	100, 110
	shawm	80, 82, 83, 112	19
	Sheard, Trumpeter,	106	
	Sheard's, Trumpeter, cornet		103
	shofar	115–116, 119	119
	Shrider, Christopher	61	
	signum	40	
	Smith, Father	58–59, 60, 80	
	Snetzler, Johann	61	
	Snowdon, Jasper	39	
	Society of College Youths	39	
	spokepipe	*see* pitchpipe	
	Stockhorn	82	
	stops organ	*see* organ	
	strings	9, 13, 68 et seq., 86, 109	*see under* individual instruments
	synagogue	12, 30, 117, 118	
T	tabor	7, 16, 34, 87, 96	7, 17, 87
	Tallis, Thomas	21, 23	
	tambourine	95, 101, 102	97, 116
	telyn	75–76	34
	tenor horn	104–105	107
	theorboe	70	
	timbrel	9, 95, 96, 114, 115	
	tof	115	116
	tongs	99, 101	
	tools as instruments	99–100	
	tracker action	33, 66	47
	Tractarians	31	
	tromba marina	73–74	73
	trombone	103, 104, 105, 106, 109–110	31, 106
	trumscheit	73	
	trumpet:	8, 70, 103, 104, 111–112, 114, 115	112
	Biblical	115	117
	Tibetan	9	12
	wood	8	8
	tuba:	104	31
	tuba contrabass (double B)	104	107
	Tye, Christopher	21	
U	ugab	115	115
V	viol	69, 70–71	22
	viola	70	

		Text	Illustration
	Viol de Gamba	27, 28, 50, 69	29, 78
	violin	68, 70, 85, 88, 107, 109	26, 69, see also fiddle
	violin cello	27, 69, 70	26
	Voll, George	80	
W	Walker, J. J.	61	
	wedding music	101–102	102
	Wesley brothers	28, 69	
	Westminster Tom	36	
	Wheatstone, Sir Charles	90	
	whistle	86–87, 88	
	whistle pipes:	85 et seq.	see under individual instruments
	organ	see organ	
	Whithorn	83–84, 87	84
	William III	36, 97	
	Willis, Father	64, 66–67	
	Willis, Henry	66	
	Winchester Cathedral organ	14–15, 53–54, 67	
	Witches' Sabbath	102	
	woodwind	70, 78 et seq.	see under individual instruments
	Wren, Sir Christopher	47–48	
Z	zither	8, 102	